The

FIRST100PICKING
PATTERNSFORGUITAR

The Beginner's Guide to Perfect Fingerpicking on Guitar

JOSEPH**ALEXANDER**

FUNDAMENTAL**CHANGES**

The First 100 Picking Patterns for Guitar

The Beginner's Guide to Perfect Fingerpicking on Guitar

ISBN: 978-1-78933-354-1

Published by **www.fundamental-changes.com**

www.fundamental-changes.com

Join our Facebook Community

www.facebook.com/groups/fundamentalguitar

Instagram: **FundamentalChanges**

For over 350 Free Guitar Lessons with Videos Check Out

www.fundamental-changes.com

Cover Image Copyright: Shutterstock

Contents

About the Author

Joseph Alexander is one of the most prolific writers of modern guitar tuition methods.

He has sold over 800,000 books that have educated and inspired a generation of upcoming musicians. His uncomplicated tuition style is based around breaking down the barriers between theory and performance, and making music accessible to all.

Educated at London's Guitar Institute and Leeds College of Music, where he earned a degree in Jazz Studies, Joseph has taught thousands of students and written over 40 books on playing the guitar.

He is the managing director of *Fundamental Changes Ltd.*, a publishing company whose sole purpose is to create the highest quality music tuition books and pay excellent royalties to writers and musicians.

Fundamental Changes has published over 120 music tuition books and is currently accepting submissions from prospective authors and teachers of all instruments. Get in touch via **webcontact@fundamental-changes.com** if you'd like to work with us on a project.

Introduction

If you're a guitarist who is fairly new to the instrument, fingerpicking probably presents one of the biggest challenges to your musical development. Once your fretting hand (usually the left) is sorted, and you can confidently begin to change smoothly between basic open chords like C, F, Am and G, the next challenge is how to make these chord sequences more interesting and sound like the songs you want to play.

After you've been through the process of learning to strum any rhythm confidently (covered in my book **The First 100 Chords for Guitar**), the next stage is to introduce finger picking to decorate the chords using the right (strumming/picking) hand.

The main challenge you'll face is that now there is a whole lot more going on! You have to begin to coordinate smooth fretting hand chord changes with smaller, more intricate movements in your picking hand. So, I've written this book to help you do two things:

The first is to develop an absolutely rock-solid picking technique and to practice strategies that will help you play any picking pattern throughout any sequence of chord changes – no matter how difficult each may be.

The second is to build a whole arsenal of beautiful picking patterns you can use to make any style of music come alive on the guitar.

Of course, these beautiful picking patterns are often more suited to the acoustic guitar, but you'll find that they can easily be applied to the electric guitar too. In fact, the technique you develop here will help you to build your all-round guitar coordination and will complement any right-hand techniques you learn in the future. These could be as diverse as hybrid picking (using pick and fingers together), advanced harmonics, or even Van Halen style tapping.

The starting point it to learn the basic concepts that underpin everything you'll do as a fingerpicker. The following guidance will apply to about 90% of everything you play with your fingers, but please be aware that these rules were made to be broken. There are often good reasons to break them, from making a passage simpler to trying to emulate the sound of your favourite player.

If you're ready, let's dive in and take a look at the principles you need to become a rock-solid player.

Chapter One: Getting Started

In this section we're going to take a quick look at the essential elements you need to understand as a guitar player before diving into the skills you need to become a perfect finger picker. We'll recap how chords are written for the guitar (both as grids and tablature) and discover how we name and use each finger of the picking hand.

Left Hand Notation (How to Read Chord Diagrams)

If you're left-handed, please swap "right hand" for left hand and vice versa.

It will be very helpful if you're coming to this book with a basic understanding of how to play the most common open and barre chords on the guitar, but I'll address the main left-hand concerns when I can.

If you're just getting started, you'll find the following ideas essential to understand before progressing to the fingerpicking part of this book.

The following images show how the written notation of a chord diagram relates to where you place your fingers on the neck of the guitar to play a chord.

Always pay careful attention to which strings are to be played and which fingers are use.

The first diagram shows an empty *chord grid* or *neck diagram*. This is simply a map of the guitar neck – in this case, spanning from the open strings up to the 5th fret.

The second diagram shows you how to number the fingers of your fretting hand. If you are left-handed, the same numbers apply to your right hand

The third diagram below shows the standard way that chords are notated using chord *grids*. Each dot represents where you place a fretting finger and shows you which number finger to use.

The final diagram shows how the chord grid notation relates to where you place your fretting fingers on the guitar neck.

E A D G B E

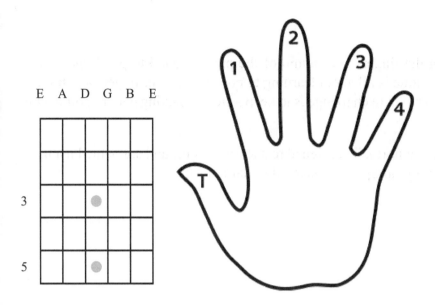

Chord Name

D Major

Open Strings

✘ Do Not Play Open String

◯ Play Open String

1 Place 1st finger

2 Place 2nd finger

3 Place 3rd finger /
Root note

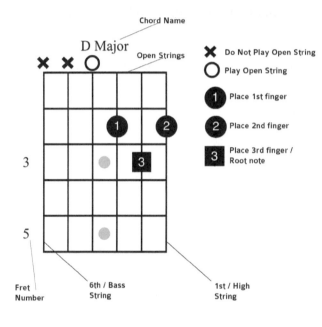

Fret
Number

6th / Bass
String

1st / High
String

Right Hand Mechanics

Fingerstyle guitar technique involves using the fingers and thumb of the picking hand to pluck the strings, rather than using a pick. Perfecting this technique is all about learning to coordinate your fingers and training them to pick the correct strings in sequence. The main challenge is to keep a steady picking pattern going while you change chords smoothly.

When you fingerpick, the thumb and fingers are normally assigned to specific strings and are named using the letters *P I M A*. This is inherited from their original Spanish classical guitar names:

p = pulgar (thumb)

i = indice (index finger)

m = medio (middle finger)

a = anular (ring finger)

In each example in this book there is a letter written alongside each note which tells you the finger to use. You'll notice that the pinkie finger has been left out, as it is not normally used in fingerstyle. If it does crop up in a piece of music, it will usually be labelled "*c*".

The diagram below illustrates a right-handed player. If you are left-handed this is simply reversed.

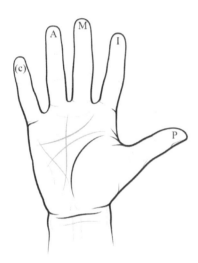

The thumb (*p*) normally plays the lowest three bass strings (E, A and D)

The index finger (*i*) normally plays the 3rd (G) string

The middle finger (*m*) normally plays the 2nd (B) string

The ring finger (*a*) normally plays the high E string

The pinkie (c) is very rarely used.

Getting the correct position

It's important to get the picking hand arm, wrist and fingers into the correct position, so that it is relaxed and the fingers are well placed to pluck the strings easily. Getting the right position ensures that each finger strikes its assigned string cleanly.

- Rest your forearm just below the elbow on the lower bout of the guitar body

- Allow your wrist to curve slightly, so you can touch the strings with your fingers

- Avoid anchoring your hand or fingers on the guitar body

You should only make contact with the strings with the very tips of your fingers. Some guitarists like to grow their nails and use them to strike the strings for a sharper, more pick-like tone.

You will see in the picture above that the thumb is placed almost on its side and you'll use its outside edge to push through the string to make it sound.

If you use the tip of your thumb, you'll push your whole hand round into an arched "spider" position, which makes playing very difficult and inaccurate.

Remember, use the tips of the fingers and the side of the thumb.

Reading Guitar Tablature

Finally, you need to understand how music is written for guitar. Most commonly you'll see guitar *tablature*. This is a very effective, quick way to show which note is played on which string, and when it should be played.

An empty line of guitar music looks like this:

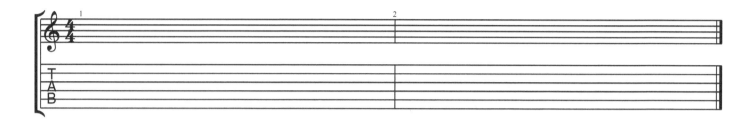

You can see the standard notation part above and the tablature part below.

The notation part consists of five lines beginning with the symbol 4/4. That's where we will place the traditional "dots" of old-style notation. Right now, we're only interested in the bottom set of *six* lines, which is the tablature part and begins with the word TAB.

Each one of these six lines represents a string on the guitar. The top (highest) line is the highest pitched string of the guitar. The bottom (lowest) line is the lowest bass string on the guitar. You can remember this by looking at the TAB symbol and thinking, T = Treble (or Top) and B = Bass.

Then, quite simply, we write on the notation the fret number of the note we want to play. For example, if I wanted you to play all the open strings on the guitar one after another from the lowest pitch to the highest, I'd write it as follows:

Example 1a:

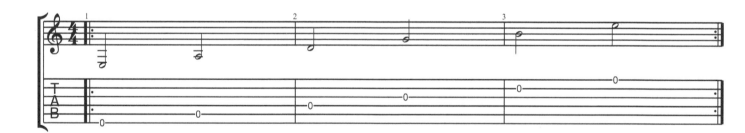

Take a moment to go to **www.fundamental-changes.com** and download the audio for this book. You'll get better much quicker if you can hear each example and play along. Learning music is all about hearing what something should sound like and copying it until you can't get it wrong.

Tablature can also show that you need to play more than one note at a time. For example, the top and bottom string of the guitar could be played at the same time, like this:

Example 1b:

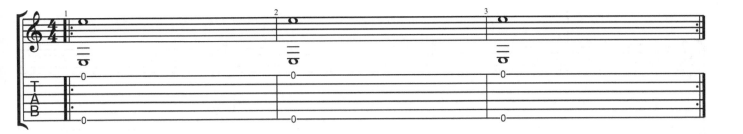

If I want you to play a fretted note, I simply write the fret number on the corresponding string. For example, in the next example you'd play the 3rd fret on the second (B) string.

Example 1c:

In the Left-Hand Notation section at the beginning of the book, we saw that a D Major chord can be written as a chord diagram like this:

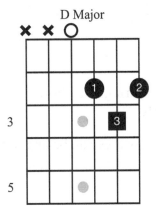

That's a great visual guide to help you fret the chord quickly, but it can also be written in Tab form like this:

Example 1d:

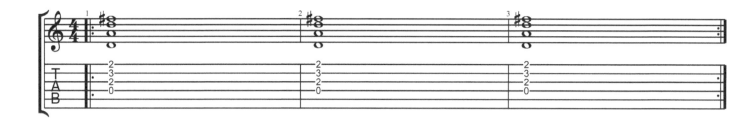

Notice that the bottom two strings aren't played. This is shown by the X's in the diagram.

The fourth string is open, then the frets 2, 3, 2 are played on the top three strings.

When it comes to finger picking, tablature is very useful because it quickly shows the *pattern* you will play with your fingers. The following example begins with me strumming a D Major chord and holding it for a bar. Notice that this notation is the same as the previous example. Then, in the second two bars, I pick the notes of the chord individually from lowest to highest and back.

Use your fingers, thumb or a pick to play the following example. Listen to the audio track and play along.

Example 1e:

So now we understand how to read a chord gird, which fingers to use when plucking the strings, and how these ideas can be written in tablature, it's time to get started and learn to fingerpick properly.

In the next chapter we'll learn some initial patterns to develop your skills and look at how they can be applied musically on the guitar.

Get the Audio

The audio files for this book are available to download for free from **www.fundamental-changes.com.** The link is in the top right-hand corner. Click on the "Guitar" link then simply select this book title from the drop-down menu and follow the instructions to get the audio.

We recommend that you download the files directly to your computer, not to your tablet, and extract them there before adding them to your media library. You can then put them onto your tablet, iPod or burn them to CD. On the download page there are instructions and we also provide technical support via the contact form.

For over 350 free guitar lessons with videos check out:

www.fundamental-changes.com

Join our free Facebook Community of Guitarists

www.facebook.com/groups/fundamentalguitar

Tag us for a share on Instagram: **FundamentalChanges**

Chapter Two: Basic Finger Picking Mechanics

Let's begin with some simple ideas to get your picking fingers moving. All the exercises in the section are played on open strings, so you don't even need to hold down a chord, but they'll sound great if you fret an E Major or G Major. If you are new to finger picking, however, I recommend that you *don't* hold a chord to begin with, as I want you to focus purely on your picking hand at this stage.

Remember, the basic rule is to use your thumb to take care of notes on the bottom three bass strings, and one picking finger for each of the top three strings.

This first example is played without holding down any chord in your fretting hand. As you can see, each string is played open (unfretted).

Place your picking hand in the relaxed position shown in the image in Chapter One.

Pick the sixth (low E) string with your thumb, then one-by-one pick the third, second, then first strings with your index, middle and ring fingers. Repeat this pattern four times playing one note per beat.

Once you can play this, set your metronome to 60 beats per minute (bpm) and play one note for each click.

If you've not downloaded the audio examples, you can do so now from **www.fundamental-changes.com**.

Pay attention to the notation part below, where you'll see the *p i m a* (thumb, index, middle, ring) fingers written next to each note. Ensure you're using the correct finger on each string. It's important to program your hand correctly, as it's difficult to unlearn bad habits later.

Finally, ensure that you only use the very tips of your picking fingers to strike the strings. Remember, you *don't* use the very tip of the thumb, you use the outside edge. Let each string ring out for as long as possible.

Example 2a:

The next example is similar but this time we descend, then ascend the same pattern. Rest for three beats when you get back to the beginning of the pattern, then repeat it in bars three and four.

Remember, you always use the same finger for each individual string. Use your thumb for the bass note, and your index, middle and ring fingers for the third, second and first strings.

Example 2b:

Now try the same thing but twice as fast. Instead of playing one note per beat, I want you to play two. You might need to slow down your metronome at first to master this.

Example 2c:

The rest of this section is going to contain plenty more examples like this. They will help you get your picking fingers under control without the distraction of playing chords. Before we continue, however, I want to take a moment to explain how you should practice these ideas with a metronome.

Each exercise is written using 1/4 notes (one note per metronome click) or 1/8th notes (two notes per metronome click).

To begin with, don't use a metronome and make sure that you can pick slowly through each pattern correctly. Use the audio to help you get the feel of the exercise but don't worry about playing in time until you are certain you're picking each note accurately.

When you're confident, set your metronome to 60bpm and play one note per click, ignoring the actual written rhythm of the exercise. Even if it is written in 1/8th notes, still play one pick per beat. This will force you to focus on the accuracy of your playing while sticking to a pulse.

The next stage is to turn off your metronome and listen to the audio track again. Read the written music along with the audio, without your guitar in your hands. Pay attention to the rhythm of the audio as you look at the notation. You can see the rhythmic markings in the top line of the music. Notice which plucks happen at the same time and which ones are sequential.

Now grab your guitar and try to play along with the track. Don't worry if it's a bit too quick at first – I just want you to try to match your playing to the sound of the music.

If the track is still too quick for you, turn it off and set your metronome to 50bpm. This is your new pulse. Play the exercise at this speed, making sure that the 1/4 notes fall on the beats and any 1/8th notes fall exactly between the beats. As your fingers become more controlled, see if you can play each exercise through three times perfectly. When you can, gradually increase the metronome speed by 8bpm each time until you reach 100bpm and beyond.

Using this strategy, you will be able to master even the most fiendish picking patterns with a little bit of patience and constructive practice.

One further word of advice is that these patterns can be a little more difficult to learn when picking open strings, due to the way the strings vibrate when unfretted. If you're not quite ready to hold down a chord, you could try gently muting the strings with your fretting hand to dampen the vibrations while you train your plucking mechanics.

Each of the exercises in this section may take you anything from a few minutes to a few days to master, but the goal is to play each one until it become *unconscious*. Later, we'll be adding chord changes and bass movement to these patterns, so they need to be programmed into your muscle memory. If you can hold a conversation with someone while picking these examples, you'll know they're deeply rooted in your body.

Let's move on with the next picking pattern.

This pattern requires you to play two strings at the same time. To do this, begin with your thumb resting on the sixth string and your ring finger resting on the first string. Squeeze both strings gently inwards and upwards and try to get them to sound simultaneously. The rest of the pattern ascends from the third string back to the first, before resting on the first string and repeating in bar two.

Example 2d:

To continue this pattern, let's descend through the strings again as we did in earlier examples. This time you don't get a rest between phrases so it might test your endurance. Go slowly and take plenty of breaks when you practice. Building muscle memory takes time and patience and you're in no hurry.

Example 2e:

Here's a similar pattern that begins with a simultaneous pluck between the sixth and third strings (with your thumb and index finger) before ascending and descending from the third to the first string and back.

As always, remember that you always use *one finger per string*: the index finger on the 3rd (G) string, middle finger on the second (B) string, and ring finger on the first (E) string. Apart from your thumb, it's rare to use a finger on more than one string.

Example 2f:

This exercise will give each of your fingers a workout and help to develop your motor control.

Play the sixth string then the third.

Play the sixth string then the second.

Play the sixth string then the first.

Play the sixth string then the second.

Repeat.

Make each picking movement smooth and relaxed to ensure each note runs into the next.

Example 2g:

Here's a similar exercise but reversing the order of the fingers.

Example 2h:

Now here's the same idea with the finger picking pattern beginning on the second string after playing the sixth.

Example 2i:

As you're probably starting to see, there are plenty of permutations you can explore, and the great news is that each one can be used as a musical pattern later when we add chords. Often whole songs are based on a single pattern, so the more work you can do to get your fingers under control now, the easier those patterns will become later. Don't worry though, we'll be adding chords to these ideas really soon.

However, if you are getting bored of playing just open strings, you can try holding down an E Major, E Minor, or G Major chord while you work through these ideas! It's important that you fret these chords very cleanly though. Make sure each note rings clearly and you're not accidentally muting strings with the underside of your fretting fingers. This is easily done and when you're finger picking, as opposed to strumming, there's nowhere for you hide an inaccuracy.

In the next few exercises we'll explore combining simultaneous plucks on more than one string-pair.

In Example 2j,

Play the sixth and third strings together (*p* and *i*)

Play the sixth and second strings together (*p* and *m*)

Play the sixth and first strings together (*p* and *a*)

Play the sixth and second strings together (*p* and *m*)

Repeat.

Each of these plucks is played as a 1/4 note (one pluck per click)

Example 2j:

Now reverse the order of the string plucks. Which do you find easier?

Example 2k:

Until now, we've only looked at patterns where the picks on the higher strings move in a sequential order, like 3 2 1 etc. However, we can create a lot of interest by alternating the order in which they're plucked.

Let's begin by looking at some ideas that are played one string at a time before adding in some simultaneous plucks later.

An important pattern to know is this one that uses the thumb to play the sixth (E) string before plucking the second, third, first and repeating. Watch your fingers and you'll see that they begin to move like the hammers inside a piano.

Example 2l:

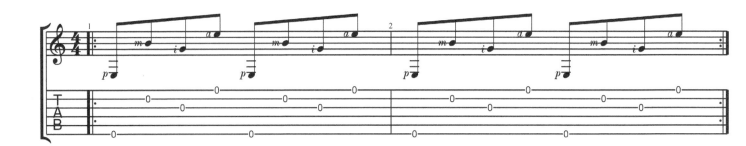

The next pattern you should learn is sixth string, first, third, then second. I find this pattern a little harder than the previous one. What do you think?

Example 2m:

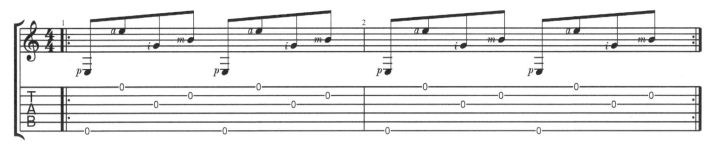

Here's another little finger twister for you. This is a bit more challenging, so you might want to come back to it later.

Example 2n:

The next exercise begins with a simultaneous pluck on the sixth and second string, then plays the third, first and third again. It's a common pattern you'll come across in many forms of music.

Remember to play the simultaneous pluck. Begin with your thumb and finger actually on the strings and squeeze inwards until they push through the strings towards each other.

Example 2o:

The next pattern is similar but begins with a simultaneous pick on the sixth and first strings.

Example 2p:

Finally, here's an idea that begins with a simultaneous pluck on the sixth and third strings. Again, this one is a little harder to control at first, so take it slowly and come back to it later if you're struggling. When you're starting out, you'll often find that patterns which require you to alternate your ring and middle finger are a bit tougher to play.

Example 2q:

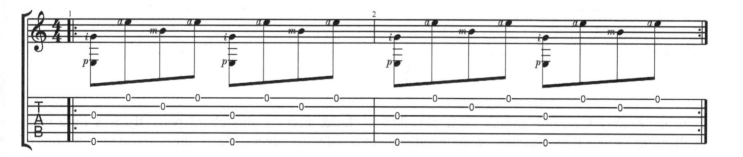

Until now we've focused heavily on patterns that develop coordination in your fingers, but now let's build some movement in your thumb.

As you know, the thumb normally takes care of any plucks on the lowest three strings and it's common to add basslines to your fingerpicking patterns by moving it between different notes.

Let's begin with an exercise that teaches you to move your thumb between the bottom three strings while your fingers pick a chord on the top strings.

Hold down an E Major chord then play the following. Notice that the tablature now contains the fretted notes on the second frets of the fifth and fourth strings.

Use your thumb and three fingers to pick the sixth, third, second and first strings together, then use your thumb to pick up and down on the lowest three strings.

Listen very carefully to the sound each note makes when you pick it. If your thumb plays any notes that are muted or dull, you'll need to adjust the position of your fretting hand so that the undersides of your fingers aren't accidentally dampening any adjacent strings.

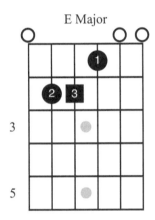

Example 2r:

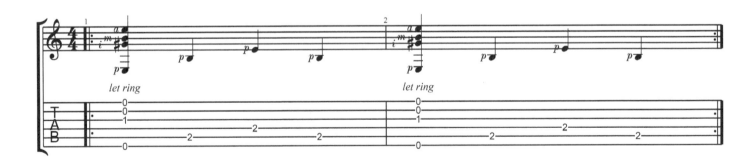

Now try exactly the same pattern using a G Major chord. Fretting this chord perfectly is a little more challenging so you'll have to pay attention to the position of your fingers. Make sure you use the very tips of your fretting hand.

The note on the second string, played with your 3rd finger, is optional.

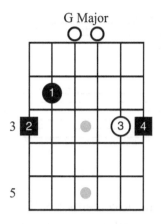

Example 2s:

Another important pattern for your thumb to master is alternating between the sixth and fourth strings. This means you have to accurately jump over the fifth string, which is often tricky at first. Play the following 1/4 note exercise on a G Major chord to develop this skill.

Example 2t:

Finally, for this section of exercises, here's a pattern that alternates between the sixth, fourth, fifth and fourth strings while holding an E Major chord.

Example 2u:

In this chapter we've covered a lot of ground and discovered many of the important movements you'll be required to make with your fingers while plucking. While this hasn't been the most exciting primer in the world, it is important to isolate these movements and develop your coordination without the distraction of having to change chords.

You may have noticed that all the patterns so far had the lowest bass note on the sixth string, so they're appropriate for any open chord with a sixth string root note (such as E Minor, E Major, G Major, or a barre chord F Major).

The good news is that it's easy to quickly convert these patterns to work on any chord with a fifth string root (like A Minor, A Major, C Major or B7 etc). All you need to do is swap that lowest thumb pluck on the sixth (E) string for a pluck on the fifth string. To show you how this works, here's Example 2l again but converted to fit an A Minor chord.

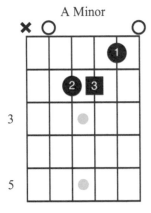

Example 2v:

Try the same pattern with any chords you know with a fifth string root, such as C Major or A Major.

When it comes to chords with the root on the fourth string, often we can use the same principle, but occasionally we'll need to alter a pattern if it uses more than just the top three strings. For now, though, apply the previous pattern to a D Major chord by moving the thumb pluck on the fifth string to the fourth.

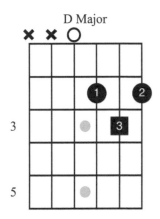

Example 2w:

Work through this chapter again and apply each of the picking exercises to an A Minor (fifth string root) and a D Major (fourth string root) chord. This will set you up perfectly for the next section where we'll be taking a look at adding chords to these picking pattern ideas.

Chapter Three: Adding Chord Changes on One String

OK, I'll admit it, I know that working through the previous chapter might not have been the most inspiring introduction to finger picking, but as a teacher, I know that developing the mechanics and muscle memory early on is the best way to master finger picking. Remember, when you're learning a new pattern the goal is to keep working on it *until you can't get it wrong*. If you're able to hold down a chord and perform a picking pattern while talking to someone, you know it's set in your muscle memory.

In this chapter you're going to learn how to add chord changes to some of the picking patterns you learnt in the previous chapter. As you may have found when you learnt to strum, the biggest challenge is to change chord smoothly and quickly without breaking rhythm and leaving a big gap between chords.

We'll begin with a simple exercise to help you learn to change chords and gradually increase the challenge until you're completely fluent.

To begin with, let's learn to change between chords that have a root on the sixth string. Two common chords you'll use all the time are G Major and E Minor, so let's start with those.

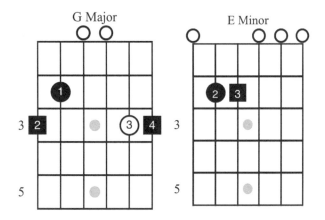

Begin by holding each chord and picking through them slowly string by string. Listen carefully to the sound of each note to make sure that none of the strings are accidentally muted by the underside of a finger. If they are, try to place your fingers more on their tips and roll your wrist so that your fingers point straight down into the fretboard. You can hear what these chords should sound like here.

Example 3a:

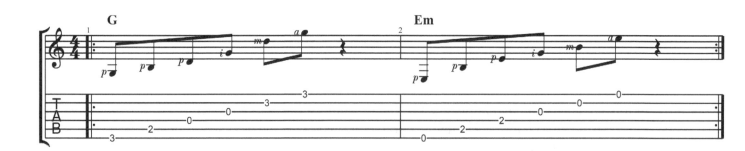

When you can play each chord cleanly, learn the following example that uses a fragment of a picking pattern on the first three beats of the bar. The gap (rest) at the end of each bar is there to give you the opportunity to change chords smoothly before the first beat of the next bar. Begin with the G Major chord, then move to the E Minor chord.

Listen to the audio track to hear how this should sound then begin playing with your metronome set to 50bpm. As you get more confident, speed up the metronome in increments of 8bpm until you reach 100bpm.

Ensure that your thumb picks the bass note, then your middle, index and then ring fingers play the correct plucks on the correct strings each time. Always use one finger per string.

Example 3b:

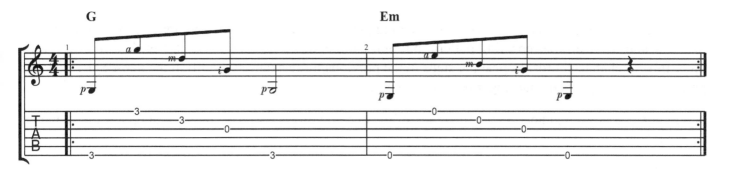

Here's the same pattern again, but this time there are an extra two notes added at the end to give you slightly less time to change chord. Again, listen to the audio and practice this beginning at 50bpm and gradually speeding up to 100bpm.

Example 3c:

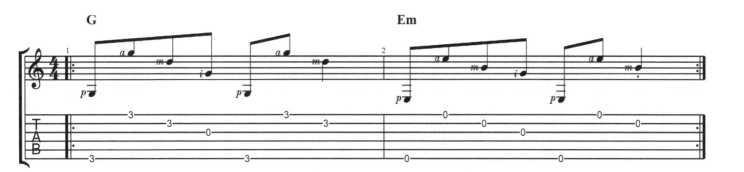

Finally, here's the complete pattern moving between G Major and E Minor without a gap. You now only have a small time in which to change chords smoothly, so as always, start slow and get the pattern perfect before speeding up. Make sure you can play the pattern perfectly three times through before increasing the speed.

Pay attention to the fact there is no fretted note on the final pluck of the bar. As you don't have to hold a finger down, you can begin moving your hand to the new chord as soon as you've played the final pluck on the sixth string.

Example 3d:

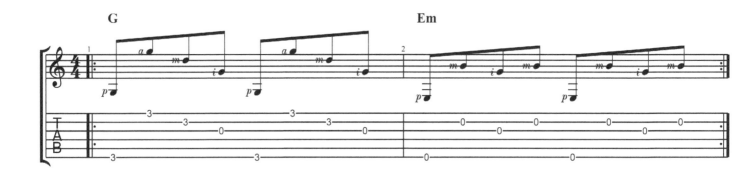

For a little extra practice, here's a new fingerpicking pattern that moves from E Minor to G Major. I've filled in the whole bar with the repeating pattern, but you can begin by pausing on beat 3 or 4 if you need a bit more time to change chords. Repeat the steps in the previous three examples to fill in the gaps. Start slow and gradually speed up when your finger picking is secure.

Again, there is no fretted note on the final pick of the bar, so you can begin to move as soon as you've played the final bass note.

Example 3e:

We'll learn a lot more picking patterns later, but for now, go back through Chapter Two and apply any of the patterns you like to the G Major to E Minor chord change. Leave gaps at the end of the bar if it's too challenging to change chords smoothly at first.

Let's move on and learn how to change chords on the fifth (A) string while keeping a picking pattern moving smoothly. From now on, I'm going to write down the whole pattern and leave it to you to leave a gap on beats 3 or 4 if you need to. As you improve, it'll be much easier to keep these patterns going through the chord changes. It's very important to begin slowly so you have enough time to change chord. Set your metronome to 50bpm as this should give you enough time to change chord on beat 4.

The two chords we will practice with are C Major and A Minor. Begin by holding each chord and picking through each note to make sure you're fretting each one cleanly. C Major is the slightly harder of the two, so if any notes are slightly muted, try dropping your thumb lower on the back of the guitar neck (down towards the floor) to help arch your fingers over the strings.

It's very important to notice that when you change chords from C Major to A Minor, you only actually move one finger. Look at the diagrams below and you'll see that all you need to do is move your third finger from the fifth string to the third string. Economical movements like this are very useful when you're learning to fingerpick, as you get to introduce chords without doing too much work in your fretting hand. This allows you to focus on your picking.

This pattern simply ascends twice through each chord, beginning on the fifth string root note and ending on the second string. Pick with your thumb on the fifth string and your index, middle then ring fingers on the remaining top three strings.

The whole pattern is written below, but feel free to leave a rest on the final beat if you need to, so that you change chord smoothly. Work with a metronome to speed things up.

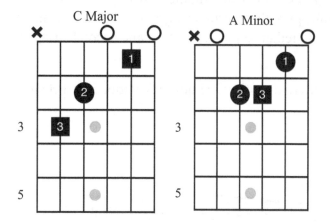

Example 3f:

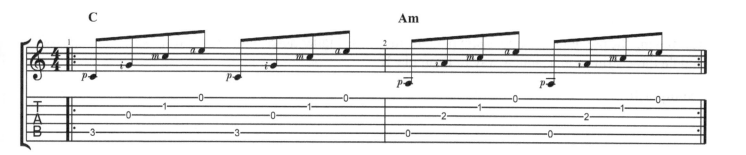

One idea we will study in more detail later is that we can often use the same picking movement on different *string groups* in the same chord.

Example 3f shows exactly the same pattern as before, but instead of playing the bass note and three top strings, you will play the bass note and the three middle strings. I know I said earlier that the thumb normally takes care of the bass notes on the bottom three strings, but in this example the fourth string isn't really a bass note and it makes a lot more sense to use your index finger to play this pattern smoothly. It's a lot easier than picking twice in a row with your thumb.

Example 3g:

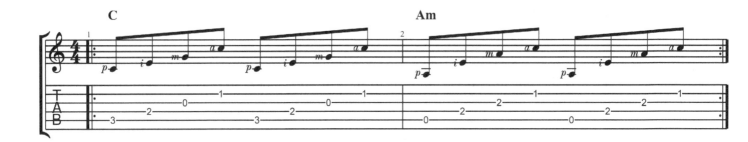

Here's one more example that introduces a simultaneous pluck with your middle and ring fingers on the third and second strings. Begin the pattern with your thumb, pick the fourth string with your index finger, then ensure that your middle and ring fingers move perfectly together to pluck the third and second strings at exactly the same time.

Practice this movement on one chord before expanding the pattern over the C Major to A Minor chord change.

Example 3h:

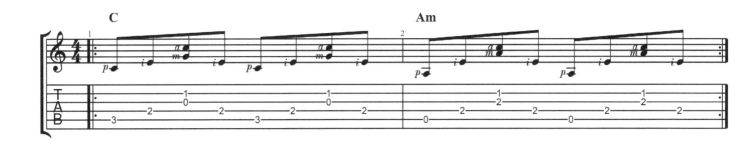

Try playing the previous example again but now move the higher notes onto the top three strings instead of the middle three strings, in a similar way to Example 3f.

Example 3i:

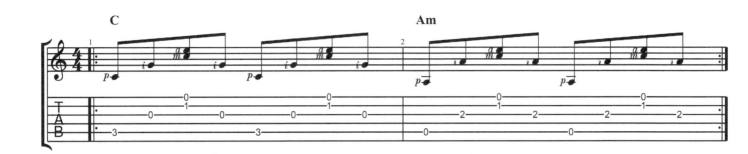

Once you've done this, you can go back through Chapter Two and apply some of those exercises to the C Major to A Minor chord changes with roots on the fifth string.

Now you're getting comfortable with changing chords with roots on the sixth and fifth strings, it's time to look at changing between chords with roots on the fourth string. An important thing to note is that when your thumb picks the bass note on the fourth string, there are only three available higher strings to assign to the chord notes. This means that picking patterns with roots on the fourth string are sometimes a bit simpler than others.

To work on your picking technique, we will use the chords D Minor and F Major 7 (usually written FMaj7).

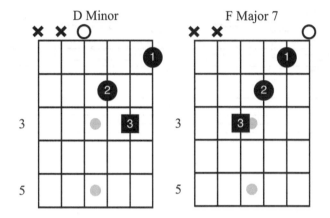

I've chosen these chords deliberately because I'm sure you remember learning the "straight" F Major chord with the barre across the first and second strings. If you're confident, by all means play F Major in the following exercises, but if you're just starting out, you'll find FMaj7 a lot easier, especially on an acoustic guitar.

If you did want to use F Major instead of FMaj7, you might find it nice to combine it with Dm7 instead of Dm to keep the first finger barre down throughout.

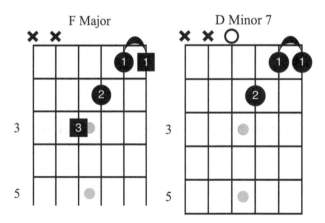

Remember, the focus of this book is on developing your finger picking ability and I don't want you struggling with your fretting hand while you're getting to grips with a new technique. I suggest you use FMaj7 and D Minor for the following exercise.

To get used to changing chords on the fourth string while keeping your picking smooth and consistent, begin with this pattern that simply ascends from the fourth to the first string.

Remember that you don't have to change between chords all at once. Pick the open fourth string on the D Minor chord before fully changing away from the FMaj7, to give you time to build the chord note by note. Notice that the 2nd fret on the third string stays down throughout, so you only need to move two fingers to change chords.

Example 3j:

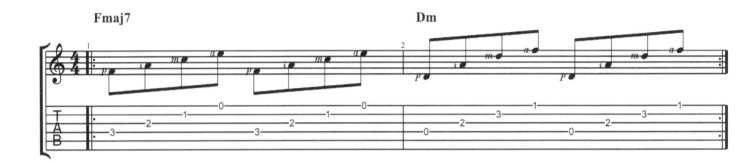

Now try this idea that reverses the finger picks after the bass note.

Example 3k:

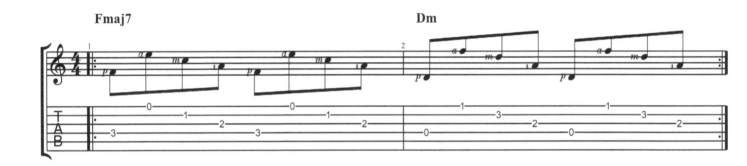

The next pattern is a little more challenging. Begin with a simultaneous pick between your thumb and middle finger on the fourth and second strings.

Example 3l:

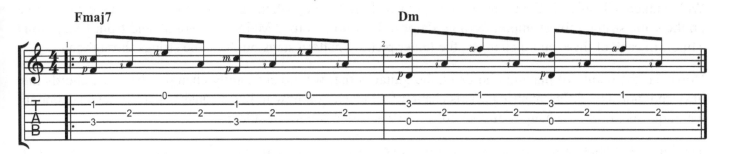

Finally, here's a pattern that combines three simultaneous picks. There are two 1/4 note picks followed by four 1/8th notes on the final two beats. This sequence is definitely quite challenging moving back from the D Minor to the FMaj7, so learn it slowly and take your time bringing it up to speed.

Example 3m:

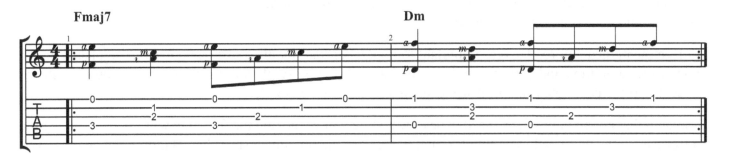

Now you're getting confident with finger picking patterns through fourth-string root chords, go back through Chapter Two and apply any patterns you like to this sequence.

Work with a metronome to get incrementally faster as you get your fingers under control.

In this chapter we've got to grips with playing consistent picking patterns and learning to stay in rhythm, while chords with root notes on the same string change. So far, we haven't worked on changing chords *across* strings. That's what we're going to focus on in the next chapter.

Chapter Four: Changing Chords Across Strings

We've taken a detailed look at how to build your picking fluency when changing chords that have a root note on the same string – for example, from G Major to E Minor, from C Major to A Minor, and from FMaj7 to D Minor. In each of these chord changes, the finger picking pattern stays on the same strings throughout.

However, the reality of playing chords on the guitar is that we are constantly changing between chords that have root notes on different strings. This chapter will teach you how to build consistent accuracy and smooth technique as the chord changes of your song move across more musical leaps.

The biggest challenge for you at first will be to consistently find and pluck the correct bass note with your thumb. The first exercises we're going to look at will help you to locate the correct bass note of every chord and move between them smoothly.

Let's begin by moving between three chords with root notes on different open strings: E Minor, A Minor and D Major. Your thumb will play the bass note on each successive string (sixth, then fifth, then fourth), and your fingers will ascend the top three strings of the guitar in order.

If you struggle to play D Major, feel free to use D Minor instead.

As your picking fingers repeat the same pattern on the top three strings, you can focus more on your thumb and make sure that you're picking the correct string in rhythm.

As I've mentioned before, it's very important to remember that not all your fingers need to be placed on the frets at the same time and you can "build" the chord while you're playing the first note on the bass string, especially if the bass note is an open string, as in the following example.

Realising that not all your fingers need to be down while you're picking the first note will give you more time to fret the whole chord, help you to relax, and make your playing much smoother. Building the chord as you play it can give you an extra 1/8th note or 1/4 note to get your fingers in position!

Remember to begin with your picking fingers in contact with the first strings they're going to strike and push through the string to sound the note.

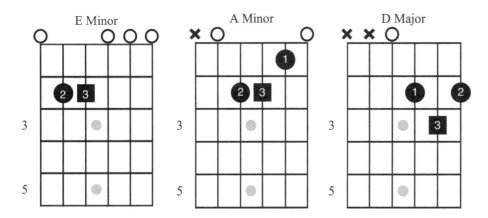

Example 4a:

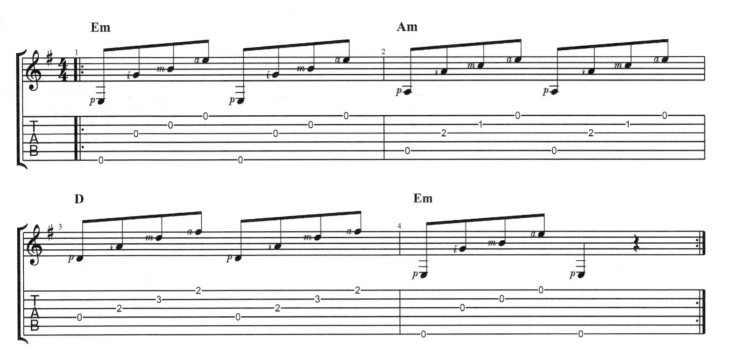

While the previous example ended back where you started, on the E Minor, this example *loops* between the E Minor, A Minor, D Major and A Minor again before repeating. You could play this example on loop forever if you liked. It's a great way to build up some stamina in your picking hand. Again, the only thing that changes in your picking hand is the note which your thumb strikes.

Example 4b:

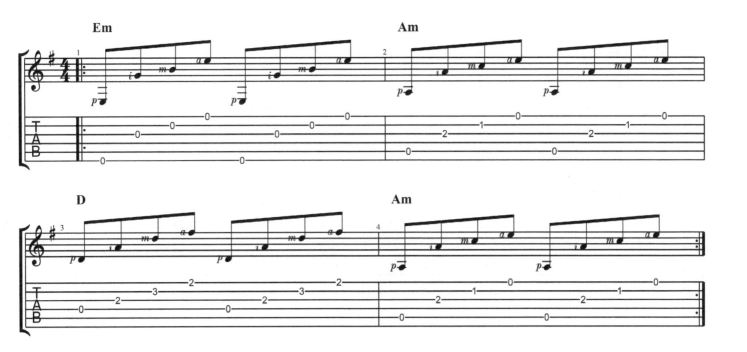

Here's a different pattern for your picking fingers on the top three strings. Practice this on the E Minor chord until you're confident, then work through the string changes.

Example 4c:

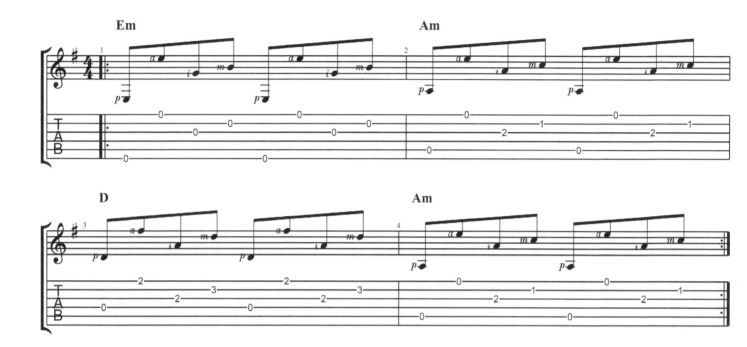

The next pattern includes two simultaneous plucks that will test your coordination.

Example 4d:

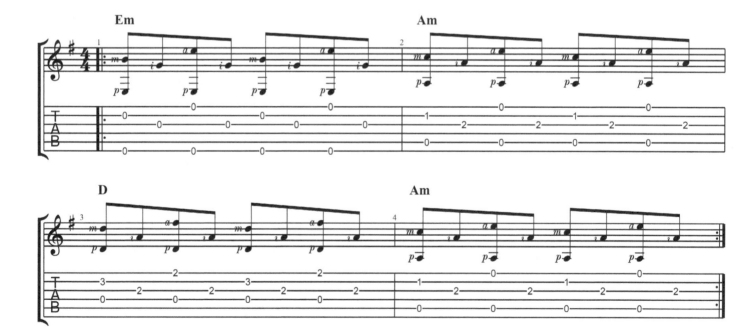

As you get more comfortable with these open string chords, it's time to look at some chords with more fretted notes. The next few examples are based around the chords of G Major, Cadd9 and Dsus4. These chords might sound quite advanced, but look at the diagrams below and see what you notice:

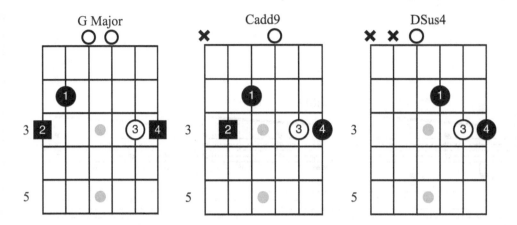

Do you see it? You can keep your third and fourth fingers down on the top two strings throughout the whole sequence. These chords are a beautiful substitution for the chords G Major, C Major and D Major, but they're much easier to play while you're learning to finger pick.

The two fretting fingers on the bass strings of G Major simply move across a string to play the same shape on the fifth and fourth strings, then you can move your first finger across to the third string to create the Dsus4 chord. If you've ever strummed *Wonderwall* by Oasis, you'll have come across the same movement.

Let's look at an uncomplicated pattern you can use while learning to move between these three strings. Play a bass pluck on beats one and three, then pick the three top strings together on beats two and four.

Example 4e:

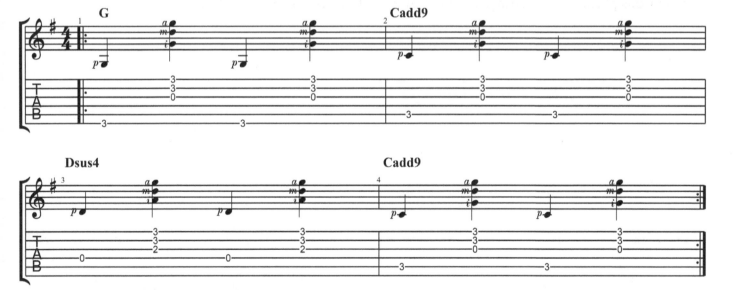

The previous picking pattern was played as 1/4 notes to get your fingers used to the movement. In the next example I want you to double the speed and play the same thing as 1/8th notes. Notice how much energy this gives to your rhythm part.

Start slow and speed up gradually, remembering to begin with your picking fingers touching the strings they're going to pluck first.

Example 4f:

Let's shift that chord sequence around now and begin on Cadd9. This will give you some practice moving between the D chord and the G chord where your thumb has to jump two strings. The pattern begins with a simultaneous pluck on three strings followed by a single pluck on the first string.

Example 4g:

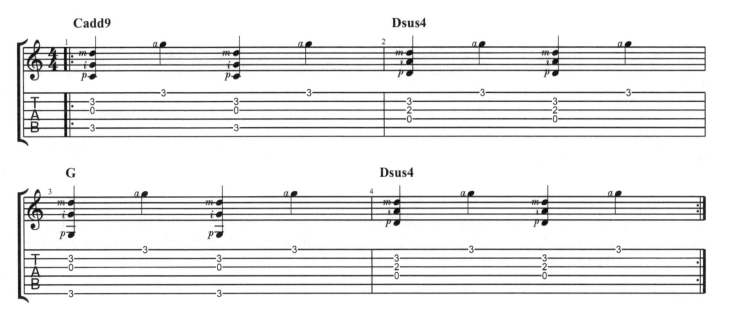

In the next example we are going to do something new and play two chords in the same bar. Your picking technique is exactly the same, but the music will feel quite different.

Play the same pattern as the previous example, but now pick in 1/8th notes instead of 1/4 notes.

Example 4h:

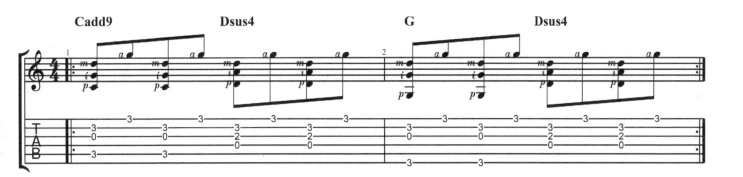

Here are some more patterns that will help you practice adding finger picking patterns to progressions with two chords per bar. Let's look at a chord sequence in the key of D Major.

Begin with a simultaneous pick on the two outside strings of each chord, then play the second and third strings together.

Example 4i:

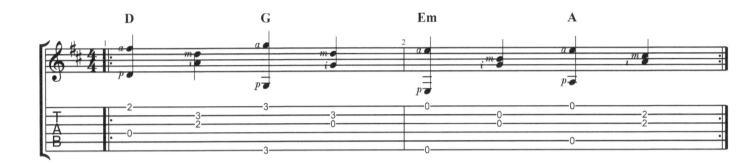

The next sequence uses the same chords in a different order. Once again, begin with a simultaneous pick on the two outside strings of each chord but this time pick through from the fourth to the first string with your index, middle then ring finger.

Example 4j:

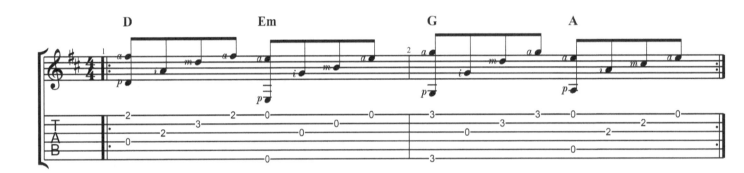

Now study this sequence that moves between D Major, G Major, D Major and A Major and shifts chords every two beats.

It begins with a simultaneous pick between the bass note and the second string, which alternates with a single pick on the third string.

Example 4k:

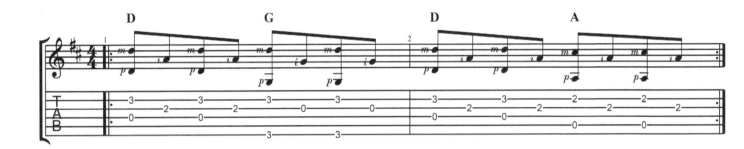

This sequence is a little more challenging and jumps between bigger chord changes. The chords are E Minor, C Major, D Major, G Major.

Begin by plucking the bass note and second string together, then play the third string with your index finger. Finally, play the bass note and first string together again.

Learn this slowly and make sure your thumb hits the correct bass note every time.

Example 41:

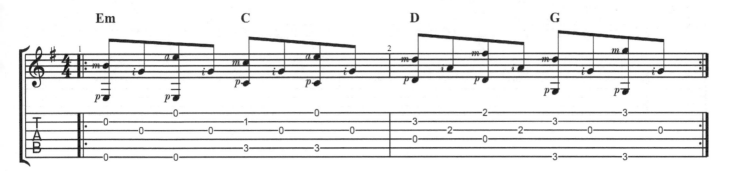

Now you're getting used to accurately changing between chords with root notes on different strings, let's look at ways we can make the finger picking patterns more interesting by changing the strings that are picked on different chords.

Changing Fingerpicking String Groups

Until now, your thumb has been playing a specific bass note (the root of the chord) and your fingers have been picking the same sequence on a regular group of strings. However, with many chords, especially the ones with root notes on the sixth and fifth strings, the fingers can play on different string groups. They can play:

The third, second and first strings

The fourth, third and second strings

Or any combination, for example the fourth, second and first strings.

In the next series of examples, you will finger picking patterns that teach you to move between these string groups. Doing this is a great way to make your patterns more interesting, longer, and even begin to pick out *melodies* on the guitar strings that complement the melody of the music.

At first, you will learn these ideas as set patterns, but before long you'll unconsciously develop the control to pick whichever string you like at will.

This first example shifts between a G Major and an E Minor chord, although at first I suggest you omit the E Minor to get the technique mastered without the distraction of the chord change.

Begin by playing the bass note on the sixth string, then use your fingers to pick up through the fourth, third and second string.

Play the bass note again then move your three fingers as a unit one string higher to pick up through the third, second and first strings.

Remember to begin playing with your fingers already in contact with the string you'll pick first. Use the unfretted bass note on the E Minor chord to your advantage by allowing you more time to change chord.

Example 4m:

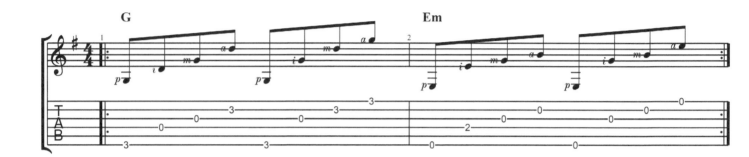

Here's the same idea moving between two new chords with roots on the fifth string – CMaj7 and Asus2 – to create a light, airy vibe. Use the same pattern but now begin with your thumb on the fifth string.

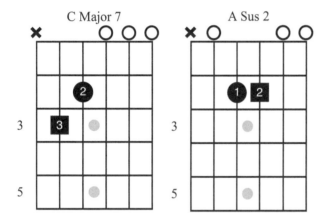

Example 4n:

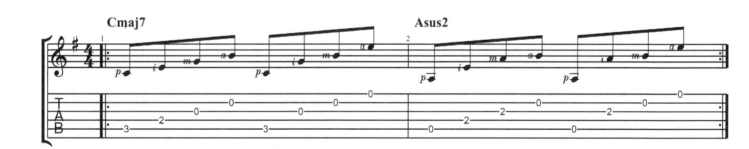

Let's combine the fingerpicking movement with a chord change with roots notes on the sixth and fifth strings.

In the following example, you'll play the same picking pattern, but you'll move between the chords of G Major and Cadd9.

Example 4o:

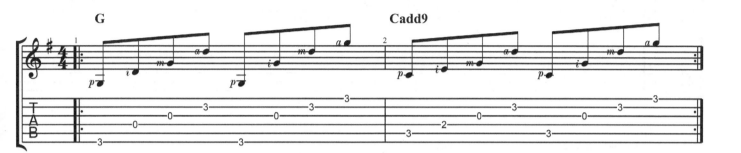

Finally, use the same pattern to combine the chords of G Major, Cadd9, E Minor, and A Minor. Begin with your fingers in contact with the correct strings and ensure that your thumb plays the correct bass note throughout. As before, your picking fingers change string groups twice on each chord. This sequence is quite challenging, so go slow and learn it accurately before speeding up slowly.

Listen to the audio before playing this example to hear how it should sound.

Example 4p:

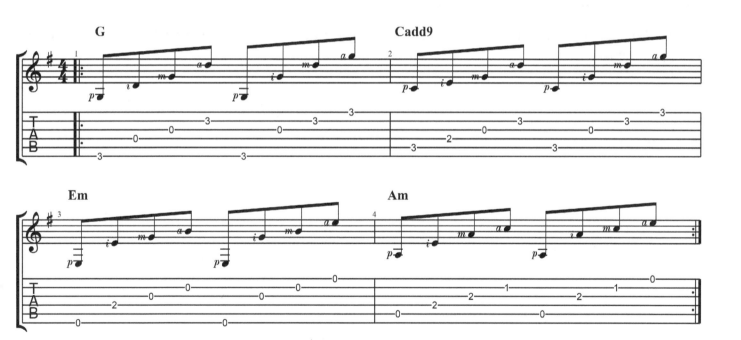

The next sequence places the picking fingers on the fourth, third and second strings for the G Major chord before they move onto the top three strings for the Cadd9 and Dsus4 chords.

Begin with a simultaneous pick between the sixth and second string, then alternate between the fourth and third.

Example 4q:

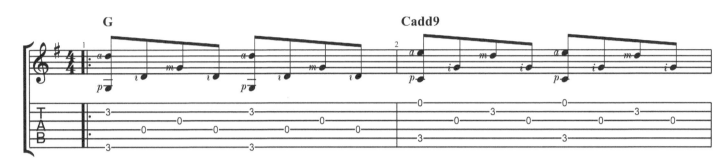

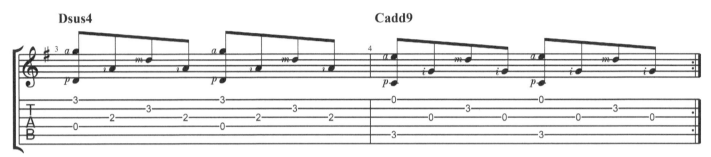

The following pattern is very similar but notice how I omit the second string until I'm forced to play it on the Dsus4 chord. Before playing this example, place your thumb on the sixth string, ring on the third, then your index and middle on the third and fourth strings.

Use the same pattern with the thumb on the fifth string for Cadd9, then move everything onto the top four strings for DSus4.

Example 4r:

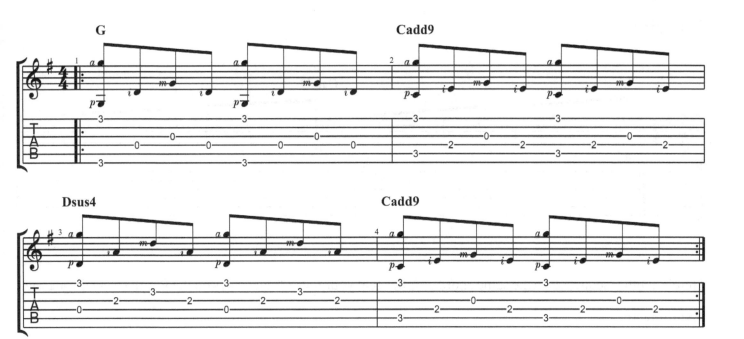

This idea combines two sets of simultaneous picks that alternate between the top three-string group and one on the fourth, second and third strings.

On the G Major chord, pick the bass and second string together, then pick the third and fourth strings together. Repeat this pattern but play it on the top three strings, keeping the bass note on the sixth string.

You should be able to figure out how to repeat this pattern on the Cadd9 chord by now.

Example 4s:

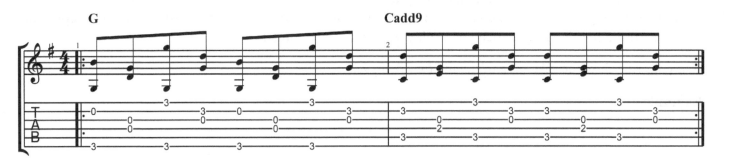

Now you're getting to grips with moving your fingers between strings, let's look at how we can start to create 1/8th note patterns that move between the four available high strings.

Play this first idea on a G Major chord and use your ring finger to play the picks on the top two strings. Begin with your fingers in contact with the first few strings that you'll pick. When you can play the pattern on the G Major chord, add in the Cadd9.

(I know I'm using the same chords a lot! If you get bored, change them, but to begin with I want you to focus just on your picking hand, not on difficult chord changes).

Example 4t:

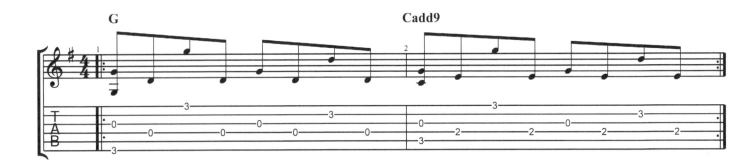

Here's another sequence on the same chords. Notice that your index finger stays on the fourth string throughout.

Example 4u:

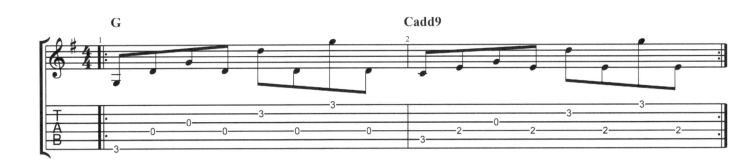

This final example uses a lot of simultaneous plucks, so pay careful attention to the notation – it's a bit of a finger twister. Begin with your thumb placed on the sixth string and index on the third. The pattern repeatedly bounces off the fourth string, which you'll play with your index finger.

Use your ring finger to take care of the top two strings,

Example 4v:

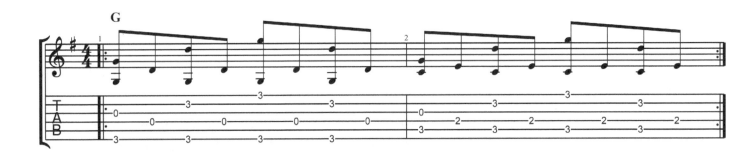

In this chapter you've learned a bit more about how to move your fingers freely between the top four strings, both by changing string groups as the chords change across strings, and by alternating string groups while holding down a chord for a bit longer.

It's time for you to make up some of your own!

See if you can create some of your own patterns using the ideas in this chapter. There are quite a few options now: you can keep your fingers on the same melody string group while the chords change, move between different three-string groups, or combine them into more intricate patterns. We'll look at adding more interesting rhythms later, but for now stick to 1/4 notes and 1/8th notes and see what you can come up with.

Add different chords and try playing different patterns on different sequences from songs that you can already strum.

The next thing to learn is that it's not just your fingers that can move between string groups. In fact, there's a huge amount you can do with your thumb too – from country-style *alternating bass* to adding *melodic basslines* between chords. In the next chapter, you're going to learn how to add movement on the bass strings while keeping the finger picking pattern going on the top strings.

When you're ready, dive in!

Chapter Five: Fingerpicking Basslines

As you've seen already, there are plenty of ways to create fingerpicking patterns on the top "melody" strings of the guitar and, until now, our thumb hasn't had all that much to do. So, in this chapter we're going to learn how to add two types of bassline to a chord progression.

The first type of bassline is one that melodically connects the root notes of two successive chords and is normally formed by adding a scale note on a bass string with your thumb.

As you probably know, there are certain chord movements that occur over and over again when playing songs on the guitar, so we'll start by learning to connect some of the most common ones using a simple finger picking pattern, before adding more intricate ideas later.

For the next few examples, we are going to use the same pattern. Play the bass string with your thumb, play the third string with your index finger and pluck the top two strings two strings together with your middle and ring fingers before playing the third string again. Here's that pattern demonstrated with a G Major chord.

Example 5a:

Now let's imagine that two chords in a song we're playing move from G Major to E Minor – a common sequence. Play through the picking sequence shown above for *two* beats on the G Major chord, then on beat three, adjust your fingers to play the note F# on the 2nd fret of the sixth string as shown in the diagram. Use your first finger to play this note but hold down the frets on the highest strings while you do it.

This chord is called G/F# (pronounced "G over F sharp") because it is a G Major chord with an F# note in the bass.

Change to E Minor in bar two and ensure that your thumb picks the sixth string throughout.

Listen to the audio to hear how the bass note changes throughout the two bars.

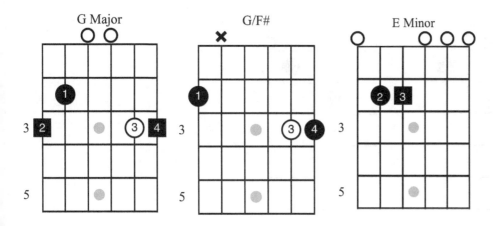

Example 5b:

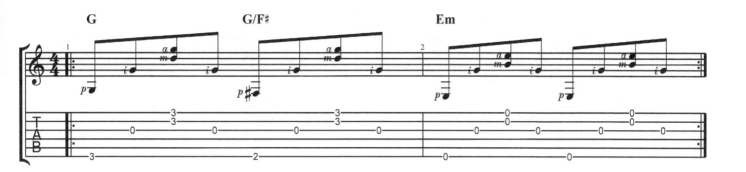

Now try beginning on E Minor and ascend via G/F# back up to G Major.

Example 5c:

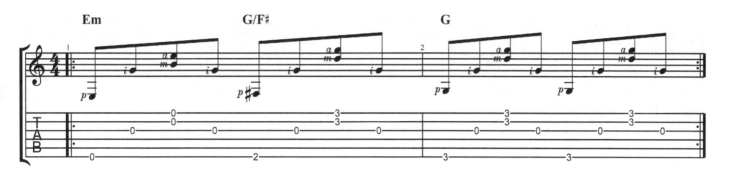

Here's the same idea, this time moving from a C Major chord via C/B to Am7.

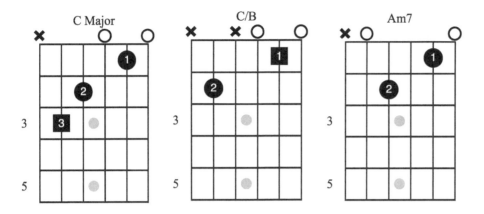

Example 5d:

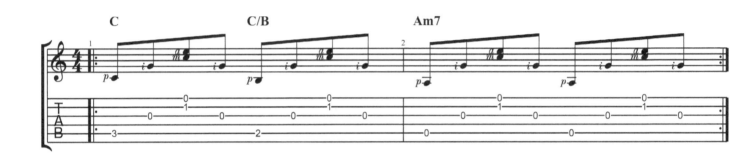

You can reverse that to ascend.

Example 5e:

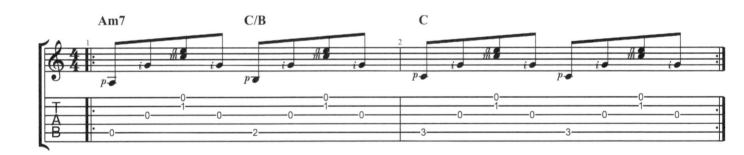

This time, let's look at that movement on the top four strings, moving from FMaj7 via FMaj7/E to D Minor. Ensure that your thumb picks the bass notes on the fourth string each time.

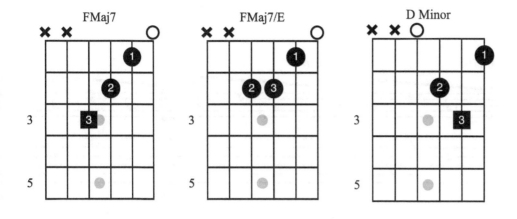

Example 5f:

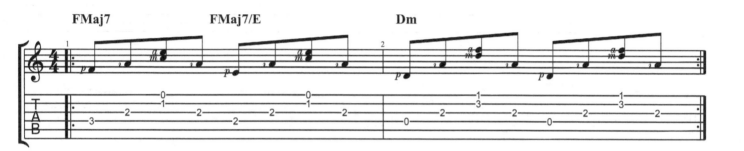

Finally, reverse that idea to ascend.

Example 5g:

The next example ties the previous ideas into a longer study. Beginning on FMaj7 we descend through all of the previous examples.

Example 5h:

When you're confident at combining these chords, it's time to start adding in a couple of different picking patterns on the melody strings. I'll keep these simple for now and demonstrate the ideas on just the G, G/F# E Minor sequence, but you should practice them on all the chords covered so far in this chapter.

Us your thumb to pick the descending bass notes on the 6th string, then use your middle, index then ring fingers to pick the pattern on the top strings.

Example 5i:

Here's the same chord sequence, but this time play the melody strings sequentially from the first to the third.

Example 5j:

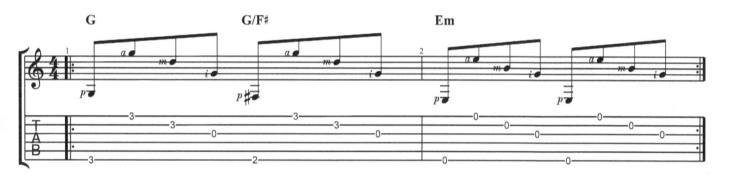

The next idea includes a double pluck on the first and second strings, then an isolated open third string played with your index finger.

Example 5k:

When you've got the previous three picking patterns under your belt, go back through earlier chapters and adapt any ideas you like to incorporate the descending basslines.

All the basslines so far have descended or ascended between chords with bass notes on the same string. Let's take a look at a couple of ways to connect chords where the bass notes move across strings.

For the following example we're going to ascend from a G Major chord to a Cadd9 chord.

Begin with the standard G Major shape and play the patten described before Example 5a. Pay attention to beat 3 in the first bar – instead of playing the bass note on the sixth string as normal, you are going to pick the note on the fifth string, second fret. You could call this chord Cadd9/B if you really wanted to!

Notice that you don't actually need to move your hand away from the G Major chord because you're already fretting the 2nd fret with your first finger. However, it is actually quite easy to accidentally mute the note with the underside of your second finger, so many people like to lift their second finger off the sixth string as they play the fifth string. From there, you will shift your bottom two fretting fingers across one string to form the Cadd9 shape.

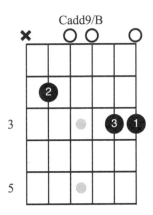

Example 5l:

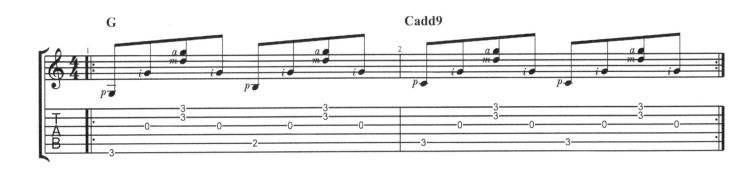

This example is identical, but instead of changing to Cadd9, you're going to move to a normal C Major chord. You'll probably find this a little bit more difficult as you need to make a very quick chord change from G Major to C Major right at the end of the bar. Focus on where your third finger will land on the fifth string, 3rd fret as you change to C Major, and "lead" with that finger.

Remember, if you can get the bass note down first, you'll give yourself a little bit of extra time to fret the rest of the chord while you pick the fifth string.

Example 5m:

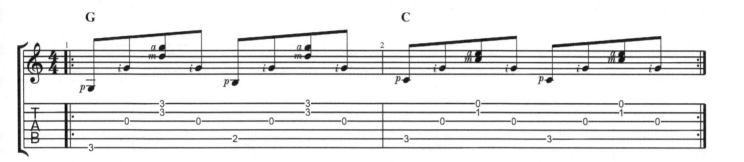

Here's that idea reversed, beginning from the C Major chord descending to G via C/B

Example 5n:

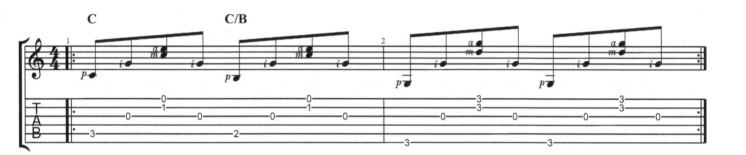

The same general idea can be used ascending from C Major to F Major or FMaj7 (C/E). The next example shows this pattern and also reverses it in the second two bars.

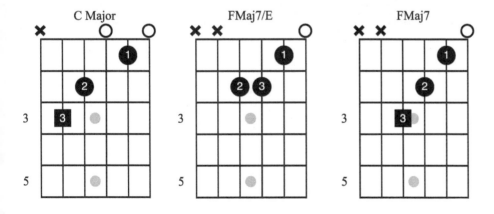

Example 5o:

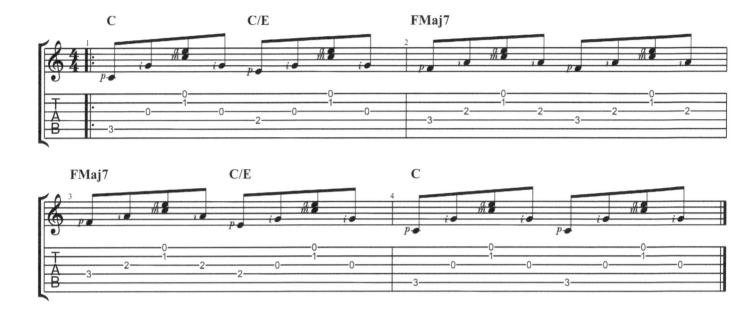

Once you've got these bass movements under your fingers, try adding some of the different fingerpicking patterns from earlier. Here are two examples of how you can combine a melodic bassline with a more interesting picking pattern.

Focus on playing the fingerpicking pattern perfectly on one chord before adding in the basslines on the third beat of each bar.

Example 5p:

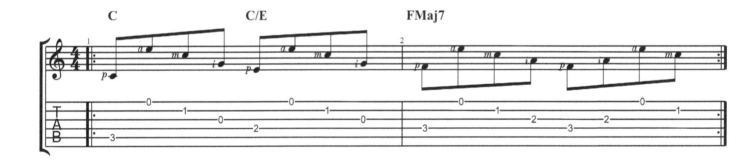

Example 5q:

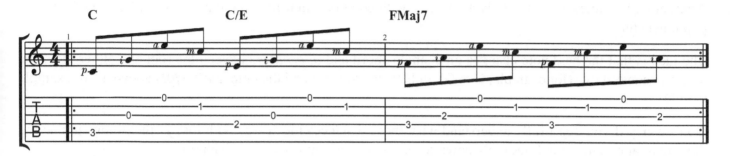

In the next chapter we're going to learn how to make your picking patterns a little more intricate and we'll come back to the idea of adding basslines to those ideas later. However, right now I just want to introduce you to the idea that it's possible to change bass note on every beat of the bar if you want to.

Again, I've simplified the picking part so you can focus on your thumb and chord changes, but check out this idea that moves between more chords and changes bass note on each beat.

Example 5r:

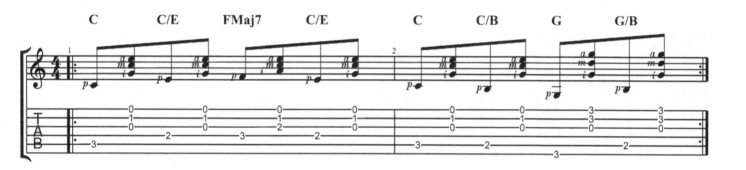

We'll come back to these melodic bass movements later, but next I want to teach you a different type of idea – the *alternating* bassline.

Chapter Six: Alternating Basslines

Alternating basslines are commonly associated with country guitar playing, but are also a feature of folk and pop music too.

The idea is that the bass note changes on a single chord and *alternates* between the root and either the same note an octave above (for example, G to G), or between the root and the note that's a *fifth* above it (for example G to D).

Don't worry if you don't fully understand what those distances mean – as with many other things in playing the guitar, alternating basslines boils down to learning some patterns on each chord.

Let's begin by learning a simple root and octave alternating bass note pattern on an E Major chord.

Hold down E Major and pick the sixth string on beats one and three, and the fourth string on beats two and four. Notice how your thumb alternates regularly between the sixth and fourth string.

Don't worry about doing anything with your picking fingers just yet.

Example 6a:

Now we can add a plucked chord on every beat using the picking fingers on the top four strings.

Example 6b:

Let's add a bit of rhythmic interest and move the chord pluck between the beats, so you're playing a bass note on the beat and the pluck on the 1/8th note in between each thumb pick. Listen to the audio to hear how this should sound if you're uncertain.

Example 6c:

In the next example, the thumb pattern is the same, but now we will add a slightly more intricate pattern in the fingers. Alternate your index and middle fingers in 1/8th notes on the third and second strings.

Example 6d:

This example extends the pattern in the picking fingers to cross all three strings. Begin on the third string, then ascend to the first and descend to the third again. This will be a little more challenging but stay with it. Pay attention to keeping your fingers in sync and notice which fingers strike the strings with each thumb pick.

Example 6e:

As you become more confident with this thumb pattern you can add more intricate picking ideas. In fact, any picking pattern, no matter how complicated, can be combined with an alternating bassline. This example is slightly more advanced but should get you moving in the right direction.

The bass is identical to before, but the rhythm and coordination of the finger picks is a little more advanced. Learn each beat as a separate unit and listen to the audio before slowly combining each unit.

Focus on the points where your thumb and fingers come together.

Example 6f:

Now you're getting to grips with that, let's look at some other alternating bass note patterns you should know.

The bass pattern I've shown you on E Major alternates between the root of the chord and its octave note on the fourth string. However, there is another important pattern you can learn here that works on any chord with a root on the sixth string.

It's possible to add a bass note on the fifth string on beat three of the bar.

Instead of picking strings 6 4 6 4 with your thumb, you will pick 6 4 5 4.

Try that now with chord finger picks on just the third and second strings on each beat. This does take a bit more concentration, but practice with a slow metronome and focus on your thumb movement. Actually look at the string you're going to pick next.

Example 6g:

Now try moving the chord picks onto the off beats between the bassline.

Example 6h:

When you're comfortable with that, bring in this slightly more intricate picking pattern, switching between the third and second string. Stay focused on landing your bass notes on the right string at the right time.

Example 6i:

This pattern will test you a little bit more. You'll stick with the 6 4 5 4 bassline, but your picking fingers will ascend and descend in 1/8th notes between the third, second and first strings. It's a bit like rubbing your tummy and patting your head, so go slowly and pay attention to where the thumb and fingers sync up. Once you have mastered this pattern, you'll be well on your way to developing perfect independence between your thumb and fingers.

Building this level of independence is very important because the goal is to have a thumbed bassline that's always perfectly placed on the beat while your fingers have the coordination and freedom to play any pattern you like.

Example 6j:

Now try this pattern with a G Major chord in isolation. You'll hear that the note played on the fifth string isn't the 5th of the scale, it's the more melodic 3rd, but that doesn't matter – it's the consistent bass pattern that's more important.

If this pattern is a challenge with the G chord, return to the easier pattern in Example 6g and build up in stages from there. You can of course still play the 6 4 6 4 pattern on a G Major chord too, so you might want to try that to hear the different effect.

Example 6k:

When it comes to playing alternating basslines with chords that have a fifth string root, the bass alternates between playing the root on the fifth string and the 5th on the sixth string.

Let's look at how this works with an A Minor chord.

Pick the fifth string with your thumb then pluck the fourth, third and second strings together with your fingers. To play the alternating bass, pick the sixth string then pluck the chord again. Repeat this pattern to create the alternating bassline. You'll hear that this sounds very "country".

Most people find this pattern a bit more challenging than playing alternate bass notes on chords with a sixth string root because it can feel like your thumb is going in a different direction to your fingers. Stick with it, increase the speed slowly and you'll get there!

Example 6l:

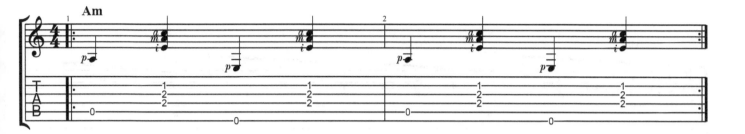

Now add a simple pattern with the plucking fingers while you keep the bass notes alternating with your thumb.

Example 6m:

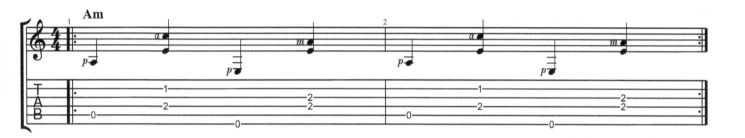

Here's a slightly more intricate idea.

Example 6n:

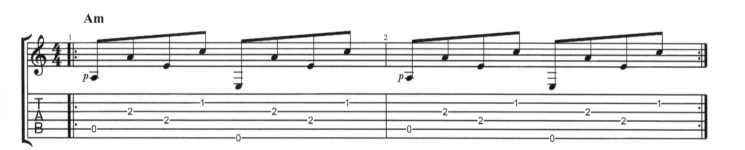

This idea is a little harder.

Example 6o:

A Minor has a root on the open fifth string, which means that you don't have to use a finger to fret this note. However, most chords don't have convenient open strings, so you need to learn how to create an alternating bassline with a chord that has a fretted bass note.

Let's see how the alternating bass is created on a chord like C Major.

When playing chords with a fifth string root, you need to move your finger from the root note to the note on the sixth string that's directly adjacent to it. For example, with C Major, the root is on the 3rd fret of the fifth string, so the alternating bass note is the 3rd fret on the sixth string. This means that you must move the finger playing the root note between the two strings. Example 6p will show you how.

Hold down the C Major chord and begin by picking the fifth string before plucking the fourth, third and second strings. Move your third finger across from the 3rd fret root on the fifth string and place it on the 3rd fret of the sixth string. Pick this note then pluck the chord again.

Listen carefully to the sound of every pick. Ensure nothing is muted and you're sounding only the strings you want to play.

Example 6p:

Again, let's add a little bit of interest to the picking fingers

Example 6q:

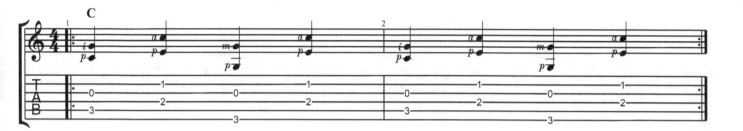

And now let's create an 1/8th note pattern.

Example 6r:

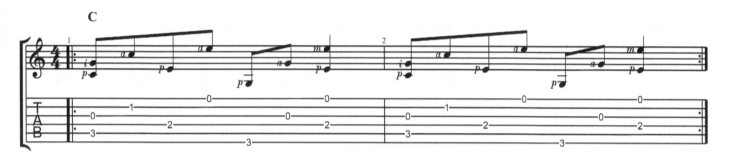

Work with these patterns until the movement in your thumb is completely unconscious. A good test is to see if you can speak to someone while playing Example 6p.

Now you're starting to get this alternating bass pattern under your fingers, it's time to practice moving smoothly from C Major to A Minor. Return to the simple "chord pluck" pattern from earlier and play two bars of C Major before changing to A Minor in 1/4 notes.

Example 6s:

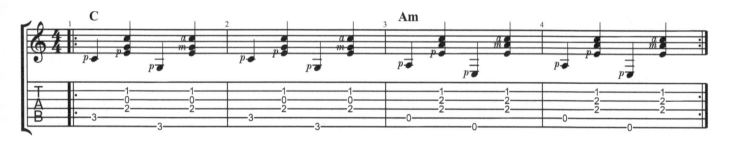

Repeat that idea and add a simple picking pattern.

Example 6t:

As your confidence builds, go back to the earlier chapters and pick out a few patterns you enjoy. Add them to the alternating bass movements between C Major and A Minor.

The good news is that once you've mastered this bass movement, it's exactly the same idea when you play chords with a fourth string root note.

Here's that pattern with a D Major chord. Notice that the thumb moves between the open fourth and open fifth strings.

Example 6u:

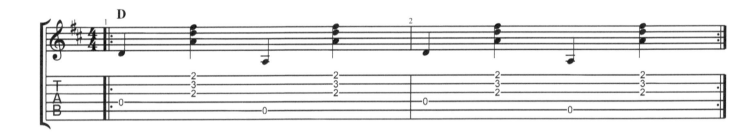

Now here's the same idea with an FMaj7 chord.

Example 6v:

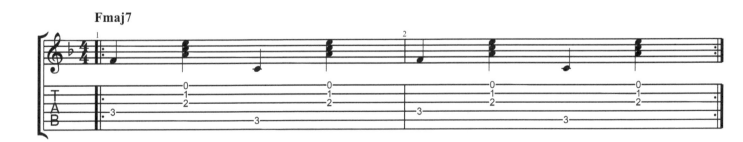

This example links FMaj7 to D Minor.

Example 6w:

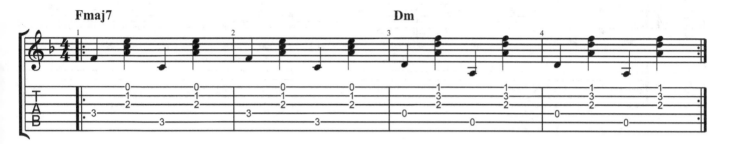

I'll leave it to you to start adding in a few finger picking patterns. Begin with the ones we looked at with C Major, then go through the book and find some of your own. Soon we're going to look at how to make these finger picking ideas much more inventive!

One challenge you'll come across is changing between the root to fourth string pattern of a G Major or E Minor chord, and the fifth string to sixth string pattern of a C Major or A Minor chord. The reason for this is because the direction of the thumb movement changes. To practice this idea, here's a simple pattern that moves between E Minor and C Major. Learn it slowly and concentrate on every single thumb pick. As you get this basic idea together, add in some more adventurous finger picking ideas.

Example 6x:

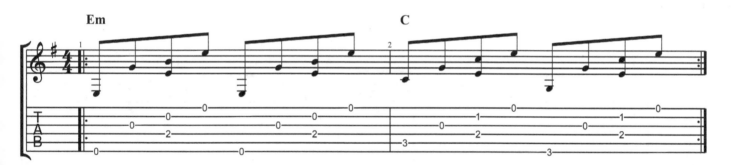

The final examples in this chapter show three different open chord sequences that combine alternating bass notes with finger picking patterns on the melody strings. The most difficult part of any sequence comes when it's time to change chord, so make sure you master the picking pattern and bassline.

Example 6y:

Example 6z:

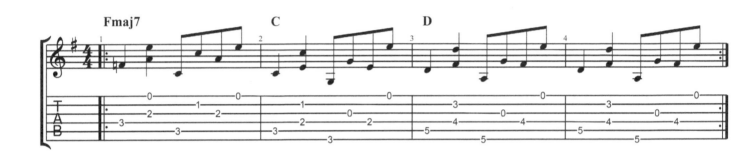

Example 6z1:

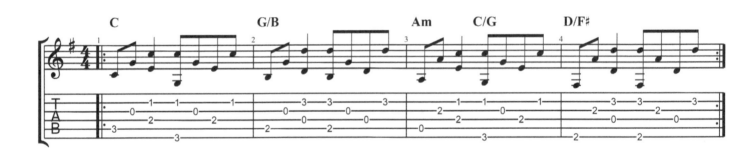

Now you're starting to develop some more control over your thumb, it's time to start adding some quicker notes to the finger picking patterns by introducing 1/16th notes. You'll quickly discover that even the most intricate of patterns can be broken down quite simply and you'll be playing like a pro in no time!

Chapter Seven: Introducing 1/16th notes

In the previous chapters we've covered the basic principles of finger picking, but now it's time to get a little more advanced.

All the picking patterns we've looked at until this point have contained just 1/4 notes (one note per beat) and 1/8th notes (two notes per beat). In this chapter we're going to introduce 1/16th notes – a rhythmic division that allows us to play up to four notes per beat. As you might imagine, this gives us access to an almost unlimited number of permutations. Once you've got the technique of playing 1/16th note rhythms under your fingers, you'll quickly start playing and *creating* your own picking patterns with ease.

Let's begin with some exercises to get you used to the *feel* of playing 1/16th notes.

Example 7a is played on a G Major chord and your thumb will pluck the sixth string on every beat. Set your metronome to 60bpm and tap your foot. Every time you tap your foot, your thumb should be picking the sixth string.

Begin by playing the sixth and third strings together on beat one, then ascend up and down the melody strings in 1/16th notes. Your thumb and index finger will play the sixth and third strings together on every beat. It's important you listen to the audio example to hear how this sounds.

Example 7a:

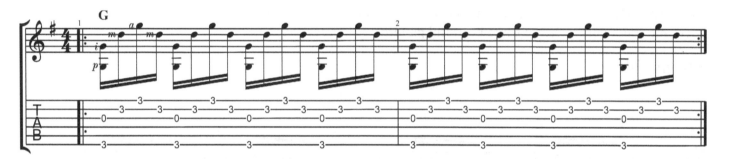

To improve the control of your picking fingers, reverse this patten and play the sixth and first strings together. Most people find this slightly more awkward.

Example 7b:

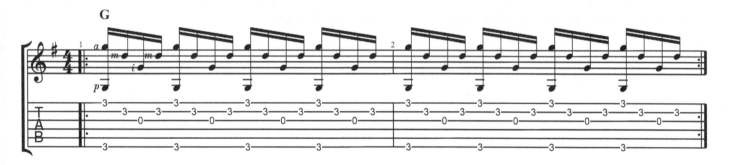

In the next pattern, begin on the sixth and second strings, and play the second, third, first, then third string again.

Example 7c:

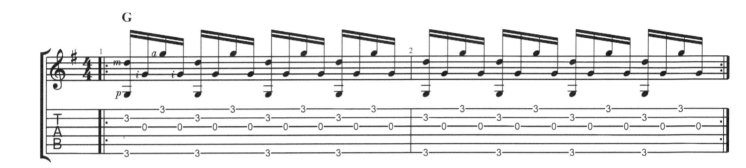

Play and adjust the previous three patterns to fit an A Major and a D Major chord. Where possible, try playing the picking patterns on different three-string groups within the chords.

The previous three examples are a bit of a workout and sound quite busy because you're playing four 1/16th notes on each beat. While this is rhythm is certainly used, it's more common to leave a bit of a breathing space in the picking pattern by combining 1/16th notes with 1/8th notes. The next rhythm combines an 1/8th note followed by two 1/16ths. Play this on a C Major chord.

These rhythms are repetitive at the moment to build your technique, but soon we will combine all these small rhythmic fragments to create some beautiful patterns.

Example 7d:

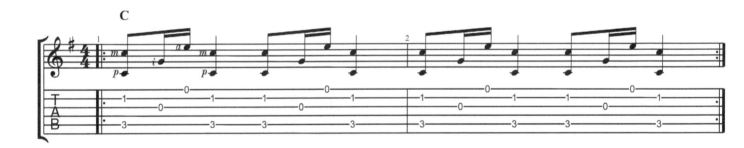

When you can play that rhythmic fingerpicking pattern, transfer it onto the chords of Cadd9 and Dsus4 individually, before combining them into a sequence in the following example.

Example 7e:

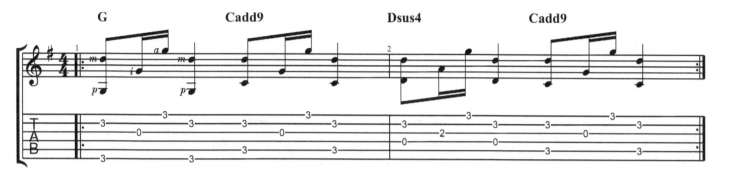

The previous picking rhythm was built from an 1/8th note followed by two 1/16ths. Let's swap that around and play two 1/16ths followed by an 1/8th. Once you can play this pattern on C Major, try it on G Major and D Major too.

Example 7f:

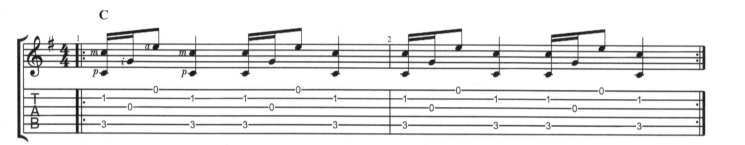

Sticking with the same chords of G Major, Cadd9 and Dsus4, take this fingerpicking pattern through the whole chord sequence. The audio will guide you if you're unsure, as the music starts to look a bit more complicated on paper.

Example 7g:

This time let's begin with a 1/16th note, place the 1/8th note in the middle, and another 1/16th at the end to add up to one whole beat of music. Again, try it on a C Major chord to get the feel of it before transferring the rhythm to other chords. Remember to keep your thumb playing the bass note on each beat. Notice how this rhythm feels quite different to the previous two.

Example 7h:

Let's extend that rhythm to our friendly G Major, Cadd9, Dsus4 progression, so you can get used to playing it while changing chords. Stay focused on hitting the bass note on each beat. Once you get the rhythm of the picking pattern in your ears, your fingers will take care of themselves.

Example 7i:

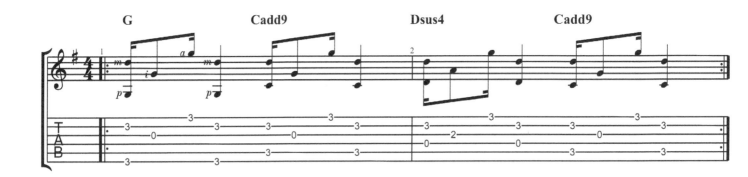

Before we move on, I want to introduce you to the concept of playing a *rest*. A rest is simply a little bit of silence we insert into our music. When it comes to finger picking, really all it boils down to is missing out a pluck. Rests are another important tool in our creative palette, as they allow us to leave a little hole in our picking pattern. They are often used instead of the first pick in a beat of music.

Let's look at an example.

Here's the rhythm from Example 7d again: an 1/8th note followed by two 1/16th notes. I've played a different fingerpicking pattern here to keep things interesting.

Example 7j:

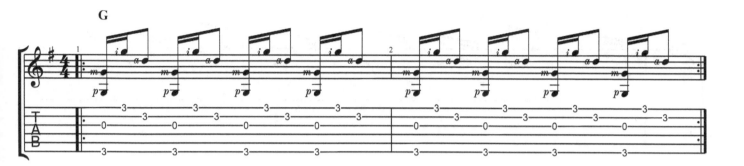

To introduce the rest, we're simply going to miss out that first pick on the third string. I've written the following sequence for you to work through but isolate the movement on the G Major chord before moving through the chord sequence of G Major, E Minor 7, Cadd9, DSus4.

Practice this sequence by picking it "correctly" with your middle and ring fingers. In a real life playing situation you might also choose to use your index and middle fingers.

Example 7k:

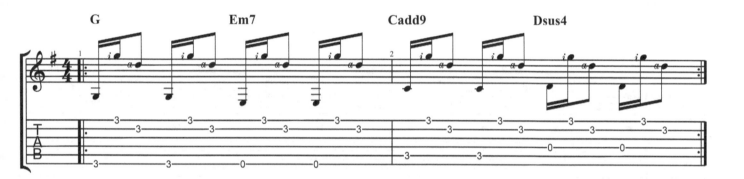

Here's a slightly longer pattern using the same rhythm. Notice that the 1/16th note picking changes between the second and third strings, and the first and third strings. Learn this pattern on a D Major chord before playing through the sequence in the examples. Feel free to play the picking pattern on different strings for each chord, or even begin to alter the pattern to create something a little more personal.

Example 7l:

Throughout the rest of this chapter we're going to begin combining the rhythmic patterns we've covered so far, but first I want to point out that just because you're playing a rest on one beat of the bar, it doesn't mean you have to play a rest on *every* beat of the bar.

The next examples build a picking pattern that uses the 1/8th, 1/16th, 1/16th rhythm twice. On beat one you play it as normal, and on beat two you miss out the first 1/8th note to leave a bit of a space in the music. Again, learn this pattern on the G Major chord before taking it through the chord sequence.

Remember that your thumb will still pick the bass note on every beat.

Example 7m:

I hope you're starting to see that by combining the five rhythmic fragments we've covered so far, we can create almost any picking pattern possible. In fact, we can combine as many or as few fragments as we like and add in rests (or "missed picks") freely to build some truly creative examples. It's worth noting though, that while we could create some very complicated ideas by combining multiple rhythmic patterns, most catchy songs use just one or two rhythms that are repetitive throughout the song.

In the following examples I'm going to begin combining just one or two rhythms to build creative patterns that could form the basis of a song. Some will contain rests, some won't, and some will be more intricate than others.

When you realise you can combine these rhythms with the freedom to pick any guitar string in any order, you'll quickly discover hundreds of patterns you could never have dreamed of. Do remember though, one thing that makes a fingerpicking pattern successful is repetition, so don't keep changing things up! Often, it's the *shape* of the picking pattern on the strings that gives the rhythm guitar its structure, so keeping the pattern the same and shifting it to other strings is a great way to add interest, while keeping a solid base for your listener to latch onto.

The next six examples combine the rhythms and rests we've been learning into longer, more intricate picking patterns. I've decided not to "force" the patterns together as an academic exercise – instead these patterns are quite natural. As you can see, they might look a little complicated on paper, so make sure you listen to the audio to hear how they should sound.

One tip for reading these is to pay attention to the *strings* the notes are played on rather than the fret numbers. The fretted notes will always be contained in the chord, so as long as you're holding the chord down correctly you only need to concentrate on picking the correct string. If you don't read rhythms particularly well, pay attention to the spacing of the notes on the strings and make sure you listen carefully to the audio track. Similar patterns may contain picked notes in one beat and rests in another, so make sure you're reading the rhythmic notation carefully.

These examples are important 1/16th note based picking patterns. I've written them with simple chords but you can apply them to any sequences you know.

Example 7n:

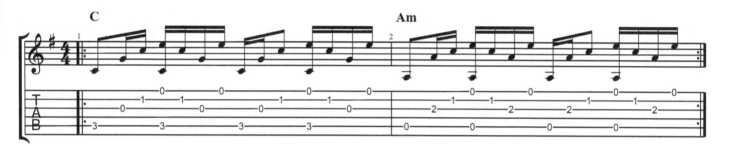

Example 7o:

Example 7p:

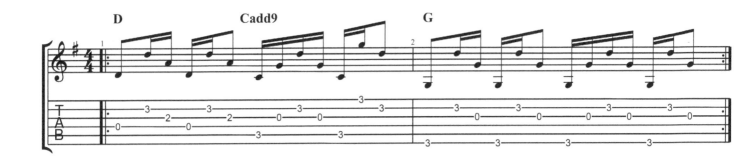

Example 7q:

Example 7r:

Example 7s:

Example 7t:

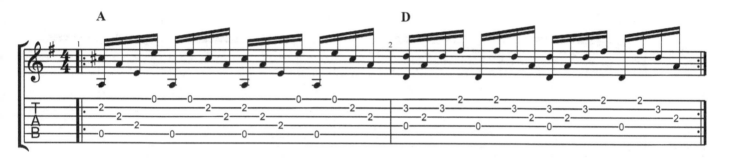

Now you're getting to grips with these 1/16th note picking patterns let's raise the bar and add in some basslines.

The following four picking ideas are a little simpler for your fingers, but your thumb needs to do a bit more work. The first three examples contain a melodic bassline that moves between chords; the next three contain an alternating bass.

Once you're worked through these examples you'll be able to add these kind of movements to almost any picking pattern freely. All you need to do is work out the bassline in advance and slowly add it to your picking pattern. Soon you'll find that you have a huge amount of independence between your thumb and fingers.

Example 7u:

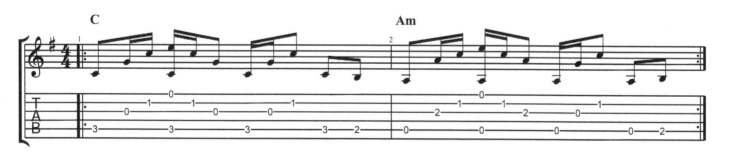

Example 7v:

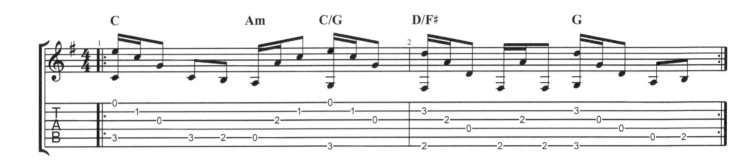

Example 7w:

Example 7x:

Example 7y:

Example 7z:

We've come a long way in this chapter! You should find that your thumb and fingers now have a lot more independence than they did before. In your practice time, I'd like you to invent some of your own picking patterns that are based around 1/16th notes and 1/18th notes. Play them with a static bassline before using some of the ideas in this chapter to add in either a melodic bassline or one that alternates.

Chapter Eight: Adding Melody

Now you're getting your fingers under control and learning to coordinate your left and right hands, I want to introduce the idea of highlighting melody notes that stand out from the main picking pattern. Often, highlighting a note is simply a case of letting it ring for a bit longer or highlighting it rhythmically. To be honest, a lot of this technique comes down to simply hearing the melody note you want to play and picking it at the top of your chords.

The best way to explain this is by jumping in and learning a few examples.

The first example is played in 1/8th notes and changes between G Major, D Major, C Major, and back to D Major. Notice how the first finger pick is on the second string, but I accent the melody note on the top string by placing it on beat two and picking it very slightly harder and letting it ring for the rest of the bar. The effect of this is to create a melody between the second and first strings that jumps out from the rest of the picking pattern.

Example 8a:

The next example is similar but notice how I bring out the melody a little more by accenting the same note on the "and" of beat four.

Example 8b:

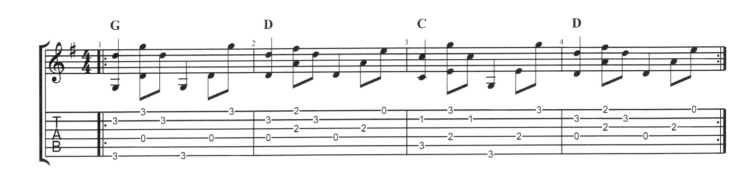

The next two examples do similar things over different chord progressions. Pay attention to the notes that are deliberately placed on off beats.

Example 8c:

Example 8d:

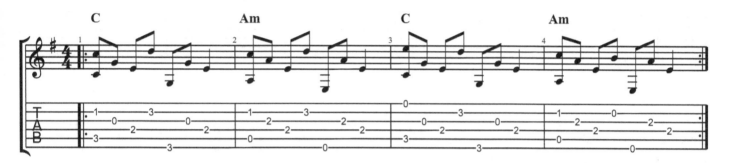

The next stage is to start adding melody notes that aren't in the chords. This is pretty much always done via the very technical technique of "adding or removing a finger"!

In the next example, I'll show you where most of the nice melody notes live around a C Major chord (in the key of C). Hold the C Major chord throughout.

The example begins by playing the C Major on beat one, then adding your 4th finger on the note G on the first string. Next, flatten your first finger to barre across the top two strings to play the note F, then return to a normal C chord to play the open E note at the top of the chord. Finally, place your third finger to play the D on the second string before returning to the original C chord and playing the 1st fret on the second string at the top of the chord.

Example 8e:

The next example shows the same idea played on the chords of F Major, E Minor, A Minor, D Minor and G Major in the key of C. I've condensed each chord into 1/4 notes to save space but learn these freely and concentrate on making each picked chord ring out.

Notice the new fingering for the G Major chord that allows you to use your first finger on the first fret. This is a common fingering for folk and country players.

Example 8f:

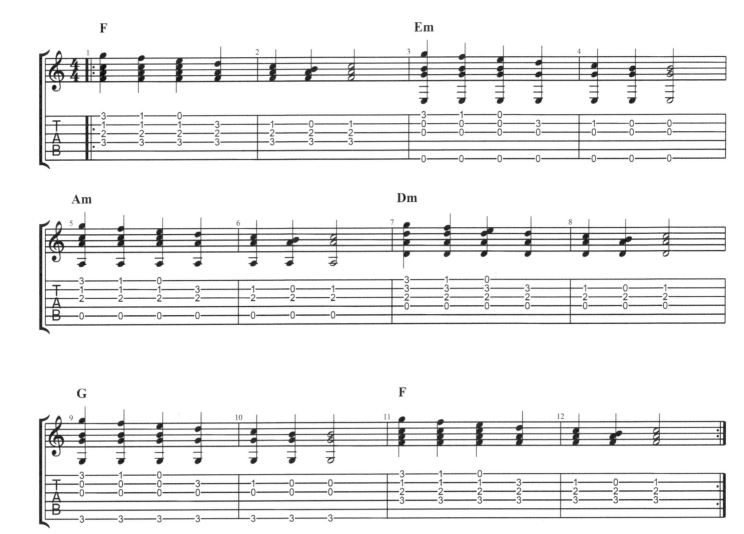

In the next example we're going to play a C Major chord using a very simple 1/16th note picking pattern on the bass and middle strings while adding a melody note on each beat. The melody note always occurs as an isolated pick played simultaneously with a bass note.

Example 8g:

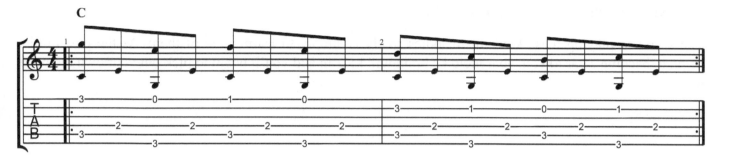

Here's a similar idea around an A Minor chord.

Example 8h:

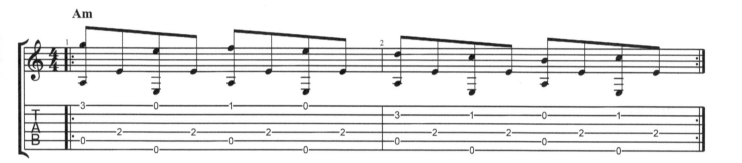

And here's a melody based around a D Minor chord. Try playing ideas like this around any chords that you know.

Example 8i:

Now you're discovering where the melody notes lie around different chords in the key of C Major, let's introduce some chord changes and picking patterns under simple melodies. There's nothing complicated melodically here, but you'll need to concentrate hard to stay in time and keep the picking pattern consistent while you accentuate the melody note on the top strings.

The secret to playing these kinds of melodies freely is simply to learn some of them. As the possibilities begin to become clear to you, your melodic brain will kick in and you'll begin to pick out your own melodies with ease.

Example 8j:

Here's another idea in the Key of C.

Example 8k:

Staying in the key of C, let's take this one stage further and combine a melody, picking pattern *and* an alternating bassline. These examples are a little more challenging but take them slowly and you'll master them in no time. The trickiest part is when you need to move two fingers on the beat – one finger to hit the melody note, and one finger to hit the bass note. Think carefully about which fingers you're going to use.

Example 8l:

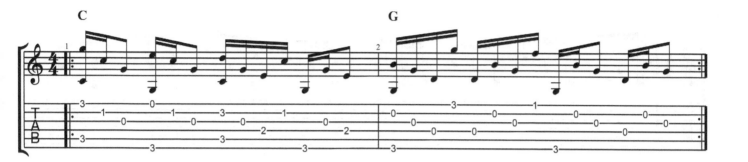

Here's a similar example, but this time the bassline is more melodic in its movement.

Example 8m:

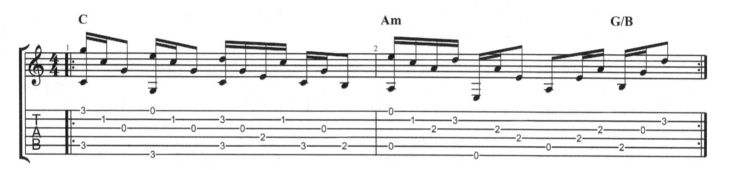

Here's another way to combine the three elements. Once you get your fingers round these examples, you'll find you have much more freedom to play what you hear in your head.

Example 8n:

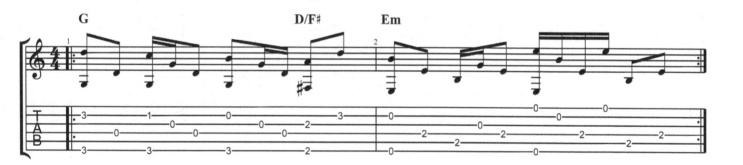

Until now, each melody note has fallen directly on a down beat. Here's an example where the melody note is played in 1/8th notes while the chords change regularly. Practice this idea and, when you feel confident, try adding an alternating bassline.

Example 8o:

The previous idea was an intermediary steppingstone to bring you to one of the most important techniques of all when it comes to adding melody notes to finger picking patterns: the *pull-off*.

Pull-offs are a challenging technique, but if you can use them to sound your melody notes it keeps your fingers free in both hands to play chords and consistent picking patterns. Listen to virtuoso players like Tommy Emmanuel and Bert Jansch and you'll hear how they use pull-offs to pick out impossible-sounding melodies while playing extremely intricate picking patterns.

Let's begin by learning to play a pull off with your fourth finger. Fret an F Major 7 chord as normal and place your fourth finger on the 3rd fret of the first string. Pluck the fourth, third, second and first strings together and pull off your fourth finger downwards towards the floor to "pick" the first string and sound the open string.

It's common for the underside of your first finger to touch and mute the first string. If this happens, ensure you are fretting with your fingertips and slide your thumb down lower on the back of the neck to arch your hand.

In the second two bars of this example I've shown the same movement with a C Major chord. Practice each movement individually then combine them smoothly.

Example 8p:

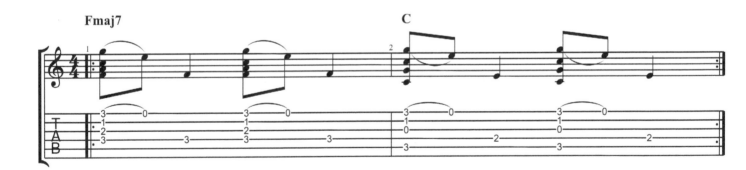

In the next example we will add a simple picking pattern to the same movement. Pick all four strings together, perform the pull off on the first string, then pick down through the second and third strings. When you repeat the movement for a second time, just pick the root and first strings.

Example 8q:

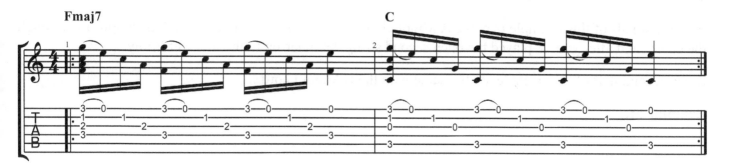

Next you'll learn to pull off with your first finger on a D Minor and A Minor chord. Use the same picking pattern as the previous example. Listen carefully to the sound you make and adjust your fingers if you hear any buzzes or muted notes.

Example 8r:

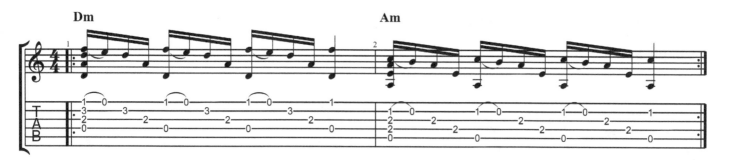

Play through all the chords you know in the open position and experiment to see where it's easy and musical to pull off to an open string.

You can also add pull-offs to sound fretted notes. In the next example I pull off from the 3rd to the 1st fret on a D Minor chord, then from the 3rd to the 1st fret on the second string of a C Major chord. Learn each movement separately before combining them into one smooth passage.

Example 8s:

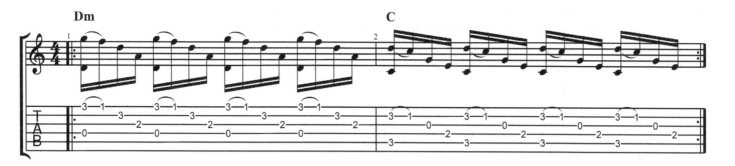

The opposite of a pull-off is a *hammer-on*. As you can probably guess, this means that you hammer a spare finger onto a string to sound a note. Sometimes this note is an addition to the chord, but sometimes we can play a chord with one of the fingers removed, then hammer on to the chord note.

In the first half of this example play the A Minor chord without the first finger fretted, pick upwards through the chord, and after you've played the open second string, hammer-on to the first fret firmly.

In the second half of the example, do the same with the C Major chord.

Example 8t:

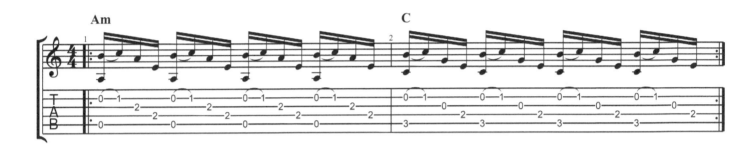

Try the same thing with the D Minor and F Major 7 chords.

Example 8u:

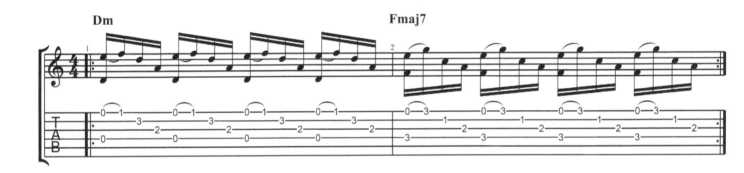

Now you've got the hang of hammer-ons, the following examples begin to combine them with pull-offs to create some more interesting melodies.

To learn them, first master the finger picking pattern and chord sequence that underpins each example by looking at the shape of the music on the tablature. Only then add in the melody notes. Notice that the G Major chords are often fingered with the third finger playing the bass note to allow the first and fourth fingers to play melody notes.

Example 8v:

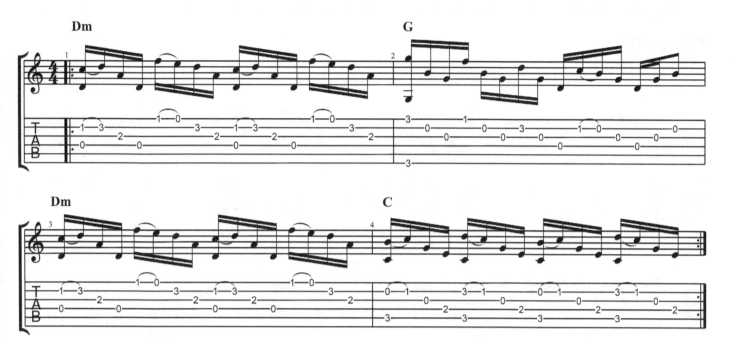

Example 8w:

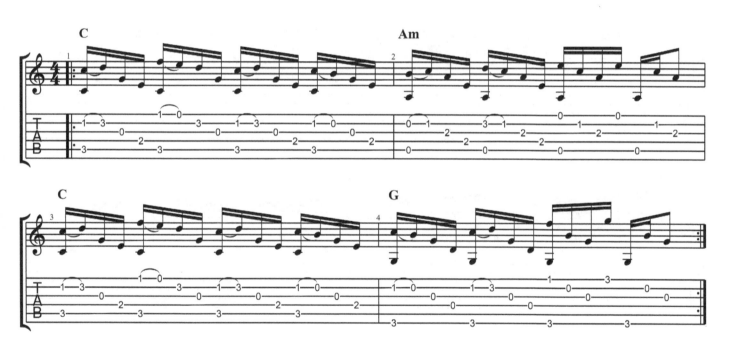

The final three examples in this chapter combine everything we've covered so far and turn them into slightly longer eight-bar etudes. I've introduced a few new rhythms in the melody and added some bassline movements too.

Again, learn the picking pattern and chord sequence by looking at the shape of the music in the tablature, then add the bassline movement before focusing on introducing the melody. Listen to the audio examples carefully, as being able to hear the music is more than half the battle when it comes to getting your fingers to play it.

Example 8x:

Example 8y:

Example 8z:

This chapter has taught you many of the important techniques that combine to create a melodic and interesting fingerpicked guitar part. You may wish to add melodies to pick out an unaccompanied guitar piece, double a singer's vocal line, or add harmony. These are all creative decisions that work together to form the backbone of a piece of music, so experimentation and listening to others for inspiration is the key to developing your own style.

Chapter Nine: Picking Patterns in 6/8

All the picking patterns in this book so far have been written in 4/4. This means that there are four strong beats in the bar that are divided into even subdivisions. When you count in 4/4, you will normally count evenly, "One and Two and Three and Four and..."

However, a lot of music isn't written in groups of four and there are other common ways to rhythmically divide music.

The time signature of 6/8 divides the bar into just *two* strong beats, each of which has *three* subdivisions.

Instead of,

"**One** and **Two** and **Three** and **Four** and..."

You count

"**One**-and-a-**two**-and-a" or "**One** two three **Four** five six", with accents on the words in bold.

Playing in 6/8 has a completely different feel to playing in 4/4.

If *Jingle Bells* is in 4/4, *Silent Night* is in 6/8.

So, if you want to finger pick in 6/8 then it's important to know some common patterns you can use. In this chapter I'm going to teach you ten ideas you can use in your own playing immediately. The first few are fairly basic, but as we progress I'll start adding in some basslines and eventually some melody too.

As always, listen to the audio before learning each example, as it will help you a great deal to know what you're aiming for.

Example 9a:

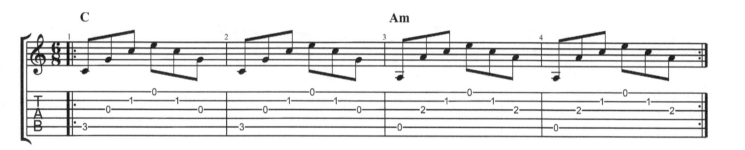

Example 9b:

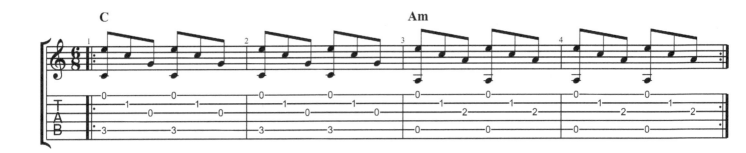

Example 9c:

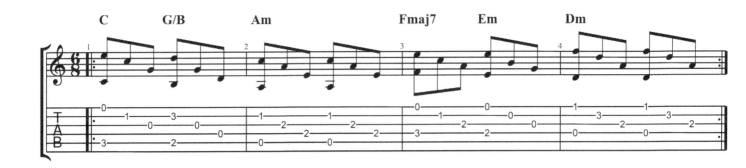

Example 9d:

Example 9e:

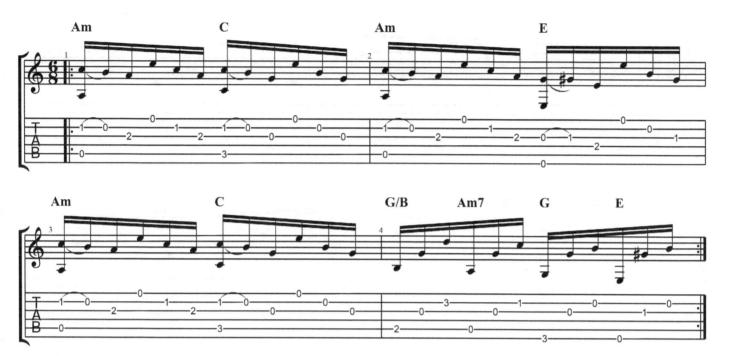

Example 9f:

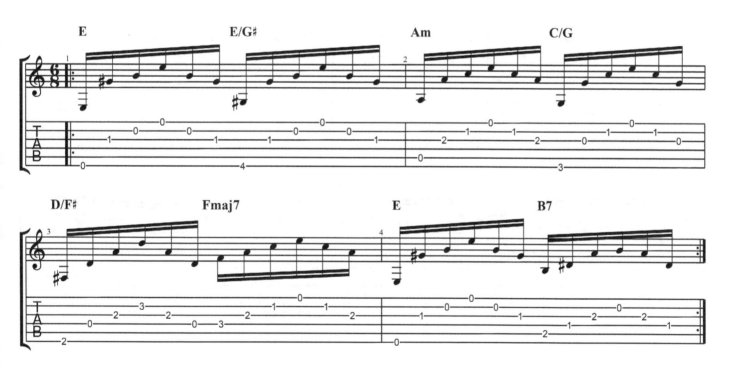

Example 9g:

Example 9h:

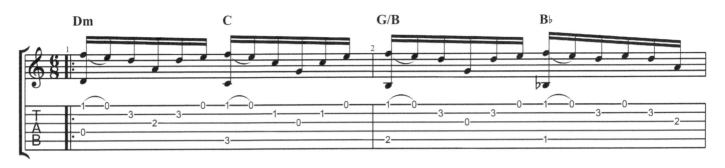

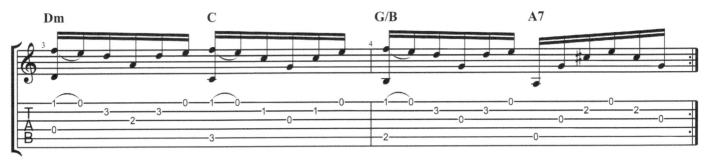

Example 9i:

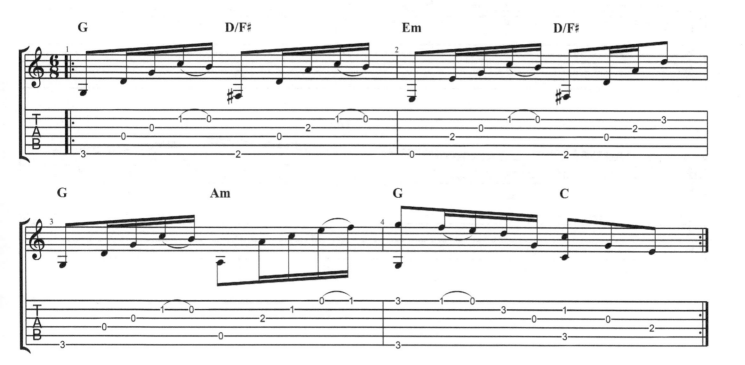

Example 9j:

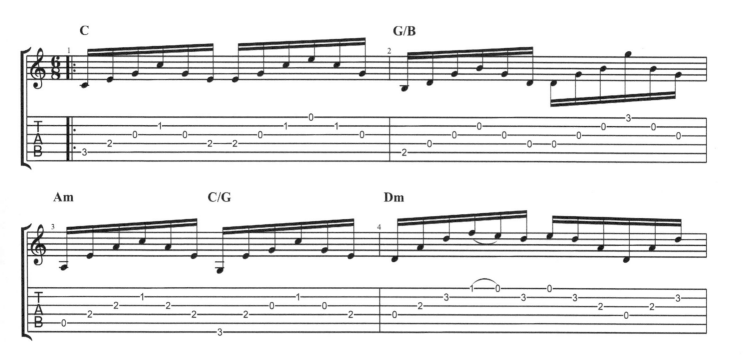

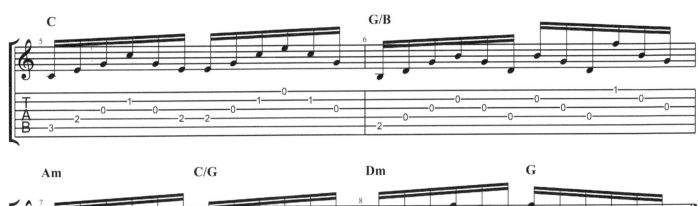

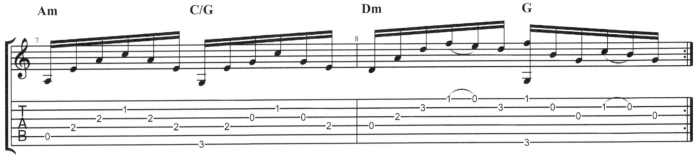

Conclusion

This book contains a wealth of information and ideas that will fast-track your finger picking success, no matter what style of music you play.

The key now is listening carefully to the artists you like and trying to emulate their style, so you can incorporate their ideas into your own playing.

There are hundreds of great fingerstyle players out there but a quick shortlist to get you started must include:

Chet Atkins	Martin Taylor
Pierre Bensusan	Merle Travis
Antoine Dufour	James Taylor
Tommy Emmanuel	Preston Read
Ed Gerhard	Doyle Dykes
Jon Gomm	Paul Simon
Michael Hedges	Lindsey Buckingham
Adrian Legg	Bert Jansch
Andy McKee	Eric Roche
Jerry Reed	Nick Drake

All of these players have an extensive back catalogue and have all contributed something unique to the art of fingerstyle.

Your next step is to learn some songs, even if they're normally just strummed, then add your own finger picked rhythm parts to them. Try introducing basslines and picking out the odd melody note. You don't have to play them all. You'll soon be creating your own beautiful rhythm parts and building your finger picking fluency.

Remember, learning anything is a case of starting slowly and getting the music right before gradually speeding up. Accuracy before speed is always the way forward.

Above all, have fun and let us know how you're getting on in our free Facebook community along with thousands of other guitarists. You can join in the fun here:

www.facebook.com/groups/fundamentalguitar

Good luck!

Joseph

Other Acoustic Guitar Books

We have plenty of other books on the art of acoustic guitar playing. Check out the recommendations below to continue your musical journey.

 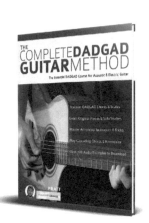  

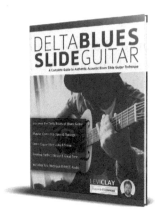 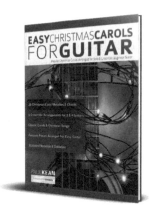 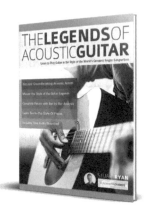

Discover more at:

https://www.fundamental-changes.com/product-category/guitar/acoustic/

Made in United States
Troutdale, OR
04/03/2024

18889674R00058